EYES ON CHINA

Today's China and her Secret Shame

Written by Max Allen
Revised Edition

ISBN: 1512274445
ISBN 13: 9781512274448

DEDICATION

To my Chinese friends: This book is dedicated to all of the wonderful and warm people of China. It is written especially for those very few Mainland Chinese who possess the positive character traits of wisdom, compassion, understanding, and humility.

My friends, you are the few, the select, and the very flower of the orient. I take off my hat and I salute you. With my pen and paper I pay tribute to you all. *You are as diamonds in a field of broken glass.*

My friends, you are so unlike those '*other*' Chinese who travel so far from their own land only to bring their bad behavior with them. You are the rare representatives of '*true*' Chinese Culture.

To the others [*the typically rude Chinese*] I offer chastisement and advice as a father would to an errant child. I pray you take to heart the spirit and content of this work. It is written with love, sometimes a *tough* love.

FOREWORD

The majority of Chinese, as a people, pose no threat to anyone except themselves. They are indeed their own worst enemies. In my decades of living in China I have made a close and careful study of these folks and that which passes for a culture.

It's with this in mind that I have come to realize their potential for self-destruction. Knowing this potential and watching their actions, I realize that somebody has got to step forward and do something to help them before it's just too late!

MY OBSERVATIONS OF CHINA'S
'NO-LONGER-SECRET' SHAME.

These people whom I love so dearly are completely alien to the west in culture and manners. It's as though a four-eyed octopus had landed on the White House Lawn in a space ship the size of a football field.

These *mostly-silly* little people are not deliberately rude, arrogant, and undisciplined. They are merely creations of Chinese Communism. They are the victims of extensive inbreeding, brainwashing, and their own naiveté.

As you read this tome, don't think of them with anger or contempt, for they are people, too. Don't look down on them with malice or contempt, for they are simply very far down the ladder of human civilization. They are certainly nothing to be afraid of.

WHY THIS BOOK?
Why I wrote this book, and why I'm writing another.

This book is not meant to be a *'poke in the eye'* for China or the Chinese people. It's not me exercising some personal wish to deride and chastise China or to pick on them in any way.

This book is meant to serve as a badly needed kick in the ass to the Communist Party of China and the overwhelming majority of apathetic and overly submissive Chinese people.

It's my hope and prayer that this book will, with ample distribution, bring great shame to The People's Republic of China and its dictatorial leadership in the eyes of the world.

So audacious are their transgressions and shameful their behavior that it will take far more than *'requests'* or *'demands'* from the civilized world to bring about badly needed reforms.

Only through public shame can reform come to this house of cards. Only then can China and her people bring about the changes so badly needed. Let this book be the instrument of their shame. It's intended, with this tome, to bring to the world a fuller spectrum of China's despicable condition.

Egregious as their crimes are and as dark as their history is, there is still room for change. If the Communist Party of China will swallow their pride, there is a light at the end of this long dark tunnel in which they lurk and from where I write.

CHAPTER 1
TAIWAN & HONG KONG
WHEN IS CHINA NOT CHINA?

Let's look at Taiwan and Hong Kong individually since they are about as *'Chinese'* as Birmingham, Alabama. They should never be mistaken as *'Chinese'*. The majority of their people refer to themselves as, *'Taiwaners'* and *'Hong Kongers'*, not *'Chinese'*.

Taiwaners are a truly international people rich in Chinese Culture and heritage. They maintain the *'real Chinese'* culture, language, and values. They keep its history and heritage alive. One can say they are *'Guardians of the Chinese Culture'*. Largely courteous and civil they are a free and independent nation.

Hong Kong is truly an international metropolis having been shaped and polished by centuries of British Civility. As opposed to the dark, insidious and indifferent rudeness, which comprise the very cornerstones of Chinese Society, Hong Kongers are a people admired worldwide for their etiquette and civility. They are indeed a *'classy'* people.

If you've ever lived near a Chinese community of size in the west, such as Vancouver, Canada you know what I am talking about. You can tell these folks from Mainland Chinese by their good manners and civility. These character traits stand in direct contrast to those of the Mainland Chinese.

Let's take a closer look at them. Taiwan first:

TAIWAN
The Republic of China

Communist China refuses to admit that Taiwan is a separate and independent nation. Fed by the relentless propaganda of a deluded dictatorship, Mainlanders continue to hope for reunification with a land that, unknown to most of them, *doesn't want to be reunified.*

YAY FREEDOM! Taiwaners are quite satisfied with self-rule, a large degree of personal freedom, and the human rights that go along with them. In this regard, Mainland Chinese live largely in a state of denial.

When met with views supporting Taiwan's independence, it's impossible to argue with the parroted and mindless retort of the majority of Mainlanders. *"I read it in the history books."* or *"I saw it on television".* or *"I read it in the papers, of course it's true."*

Along with, *"But we have too many people."* We can see the most frequently repeated *'parrot phrases'* of the Mainland Chinese people. With these robotically repeated passages they dismiss any question or critique that is not in line with the Chinese Communist Party. I call these *'Excuse Clauses'.*

How many times have I heard these? After all, to Chinese Mainlanders it's incomprehensible that their government would ever lie to or deliberately mislead them.

Call me a cynic: Such are governments everywhere. *They lie!*

The Chinese government refers to Taiwan a rogue province in rebellion. Thoroughly brain-washed, the majority of Main-landers are absolutely convinced this is true.

This Communist Party delusion flies in the face of reality and dismisses the fact that the nation of Taiwan [*The Republic of China*] has its own economy, mints its own currency, elects its own leaders, and staffs a strong and independent military.

Taiwan even goes so far as to fly her own flag and require Chinese Mainlanders to possess a visa if they want to visit their land.

Gee whiz! *"If it looks like a duck."* I guess I could be wrong.

BUT I AM NOT!

It is the official policy of Communist China that they will exercise every means at their disposal, even outright war, to *'regain their land'* in *'taking back'* Taiwan.

It is pretty well understood that, as long as Taiwan refrains from publicly declaring independence [*or hinting at it strongly*] a military action is not necessarily imminent. Beijing has become so incredibly *'thin skinned'* over this issue that any public display of the Taiwan flag anywhere in the world sends them into fist-clenching fits.

3

Such is the current state of the most troublesome of China's *'problem children'*, The Republic of China a.k.a. Taiwan.

HONG KONG
Special Autonomous Region

Through the streets of Hong Kong alone passes about twenty-eight percent of Mainland China's wealth. This money is Hong Kong's safety net, their *'airbag'* on the highway of life. Indeed, here lies absolute proof that money is power!

Beijing isn't so stupid as to attack this tax-paying cash cow so long as its behavior stays within even marginally acceptable limits and as long as the money supply remains constant.

With unparalleled cleverness and a great deal of experience in dealing with the dictators in Beijing, Hong Kong wields this economic clout with an expertise unmatched anywhere else in the world.

The government and people of Hong Kong maintain a delicate balance walking a tightrope daily. They are only too aware that the funds they generate and are their only ammunition in what is fast becoming a daily battle for freedom.

Yes, their economy is, in the end, the only reason they enjoy any of the small freedoms left them after the Communist takeover of Hong Kong.

Despite the takeover, Hong Kong remains so independent as to still require that Chinese mainlanders have a visa for entry. Like their sister, Taiwan, Hong Kong mints her own money, flies her own flag, and even elects her own local leaders.

It's this last right [*election of local leaders*] which is now in danger as Mainland China has begun to flex her muscles, pressing for a more *'Beijing Friendly'* government in Hong Kong.

The recent *'Umbrella Revolution'* protests seem to have blunted Beijing's stabs at an attempted takeover of the Hong Kong electoral process, but the future remains uncertain.

Recently, a number of independent-minded Hong Kongers have *'disappeared'* and are feared kidnapped by Mainland China. While Beijing denies complicity, many in Hong Kong believe these people have been abducted by Beijing.

Who are these people? They are independent publishers and booksellers who distribute matter which is not pre-approved by Beijing. Beijing is well within the law to exercise control of Hong Kong even though they have violated key parts of the re-occupation agreement with Great Britain and Hong Kong.

If Beijing is abducting these people and if they ever admit to it, they can always call these abductions *'arrests'* and technically be within the law. I doubt Beijing will admit any guilt [*if indeed they are guilty*] as the political fallout would be intolerable.

Note. Beijing's strategy of 'devaluation' against Hong Kong is a simple one. They have recently begun to emphasize Shanghai more and more through a very steady and slow transfer of wealth from Hong Kong to Shanghai. Once it is 'financially tolerable', Beijing will subdue and fully occupy Hong Kong. When they finally do, I fear it will be ugly!

CHAPTER 2
'HAN'DICAPPED HELL

NOT MY FIRST RODEO. I've lived all over China for a really long time. My work has taken me to most major cities and countless villages across the land. Over time I've come to know and understand these people. Sometimes I think I know them far too well!

Having forged so many friendships, I've also come to understand this strange society in which they live, work, play, disrespect one another, spit on the floor, urinate in the streets and on sidewalks, and die.

Amid the many charms and pleasures of this homogenous society are, as with any society, dark secrets and deep shames. It's these secrets and shames which, until now, have remained mostly out of the light, comfortably unseen in their places of darkness and seclusion.

This book is the first in a series in which I will outline some of China's secret shames and incredible shortcomings, shining a little light into the shadows of this dysfunctional and terribly disturbing Oriental society.

Ruled by a ruthless dictatorship, this is more than just a growing political, industrial, and military power, but a society completely alien to the west and totally estranged from decency and common sense.

When I refer to China in this text, of course, I am referring almost exclusively to the *"Han"* Communist Party of China [*CPC*] which governs the nation. The Communist Party _IS_ China. If you are not of the *'Han'* race, and are not a city-dweller, there is no possibility of ever attaining significant power or leadership.

Yes, if you're not among the *'counted few'*, you are forever doomed to the mediocrity of a *'lesser'* existence. From within the protected environment of their own little world, the Han have, by and large, managed to keep all other races and tribes in China well under foot and *'in their place.'*

NO EQUALITY. Recently the Chinese president proclaimed in a meeting with the People's Congress in Beijing, *"... and if you are not Han, you are NOT Chinese ..."* he then went on to make clear the identities of *'those living among us'* and *'the true Chinese'*. This to the roaring approval of the crowd.

Of course, the People's Congress [*China's ruling government body*] is an all-Han body. When President Xi speaks, he really *does* speak for the majority! Remember that the *'Han'* people across China give almost total support and approval to the CPC in all its policies. In the CPC they trust.

'EQUALITY' **IN CHINA.** As the Chinese become wealthier their middle-class continues to expand. Despite promising economic growth, it's still a living Hell for *anyone* physically or mentally challenged in any way. For the handicapped, it is a living hell.

SCREWED EQUALLY. For the handicapped it matters not which tribe you belong to. Race is no longer a consideration. Whatever your race may be you are *'equally screwed'!*

One could say the CPC and People of China are *'equal opportunity discriminators'.* Race doesn't matter. Being handicapped puts you at the very bottom of the CPC's priorities and society's consideration.

"PUT *'THAT'* AWAY!" In China the handicapped of all races are shunned, hidden away, and kept in the darkest shadows of their homes or institutions where nobody need look upon them.

AN ABSENCE OF HANDICAPPED HUMANITY. A walk through the nation's capital, Beijing, is all one needs do to realize that something is definitely out of kilter. As one walks along the well-manicured roads and spotlessly clean footpaths one immediately notices the absence of handicapped people.

People with aids such as wheelchairs, walkers, etc. are nowhere to be seen. In fact, this seems the case in virtually any Chinese city of size. It makes you wonder just where all the handicapped people are.

A full day of walking about and taking buses, trains, etc. around China shows the same thing and brings one to ask, "*Where are they?*"

THE NUMBERS. I am not a geneticist, nor am I an anthropologist or a mathematician, but just keep in mind the following: Due to thousands of years of inbreeding the Chinese people must be subject to a plethora of obvious physical defects and deformities of a genetic nature.

China's infamous and intense air and water pollution must also contribute to an epidemic of birth defects. Simple science tells us that the number of those who are handicapped in a population of well over a billion people must be astronomical.

Even without the shallow and depleted gene pool and the horrific levels of water and air pollution with which the Chinese struggle, there surely must still be a substantial population of the physically and mentally challenged.

AN ASTOUNDING NUMBER OF '*DEFECTIVES*. Even more frequently and severely than Britain's royal family or the residents of New England in America, the Chinese people produce an astounding number of "*imperfect*" or "*defective*" children.

I have had access to many hospitals, among them maternity hospitals both private and public, and have seen more than a '*readily explainable*' number of babies come into this world with more deformities than can be dismissed as '*by chance*'.

Newborns so afflicted are a part of everyday life in the birthing wards of Chinese hospitals. Suffice it to say that the handicapped are '*out there*'.

ACUTE MYOPIA AND BLINDNESS. Acute genetic damage is evidenced in the fact that over ninety-two percent of all Chinese aged eighteen years and older require eyesight correction for acute myopia, *near-sightedness. This statistic has been gathered from the Ministry of Health's report on Myopia in 2013.*

Despite this fact, most children don't get their first pair of eyeglasses until they are in the final years of primary school and it has become obvious they must <u>see</u> the blackboard in order to <u>read</u> it.

This delay in fitting children with eyeglasses is largely the result of fallout from the disastrous and draconian *'one-child'* and now *'two-child'* policy which the Communist Party continues to inflict with vigor upon their people.

Having only a single child for the most part, and knowing that for most there are no more babies where these came from, Mommies are especially vain and not a little bit paranoid when it comes to the state and condition of their children, especially if they are boys.

Mothers find it almost impossible to bring themselves to admit that their child has imperfections of any kind. The dangers of living your life vicariously through your child are many.

Myopia, for example is rarely addressed until it's so far advanced that it can no longer be denied. The earlier a child with myopia [*near sightedness*] is treated the better.

Yes, it looks like 'Mommy's little sugar-pants' is near-sighted. Oh, the shame and the horror.

I guess she can always jump off a bridge or find a sturdy coat hook and hang herself.' I have even seen these sick bastards turn over ten year-old children for laser eye surgery! All this for Mommy's vanity!

Eyeglass shops are as common in China as gas stations in the United States. Despite the plethora of eyeglass shops and optical accessory dealers, moms still find it difficult to admit their children need glasses.

How would you feel if your shiny new sports car had a cracked windshield and the only repair available was a big piece of red tape? Worse yet, what if this was the last car you'd ever have? Poor Mommy!

HOW ABOUT THEM CHOMPERS. Yet another challenge is the incredibly bad dental health of these people. Yes, Chinese teeth are even worse than those of the British with their *'legendary'* chompers.

A typical child in a Chinese family which can afford it will have had extensive bridgework by age sixteen. It's not uncommon to see a Han child at age seven or eight with all the teeth rotted out of his mouth.

Even with regular dental maintenance the Chinese remain doomed to long-term relationships with the dentists. In China it's said that **"doctors are silver, while dentists are gold."**

This refers to the potential income for each. A good doctor can make a good income. A good dentist can make a lot more money than a good doctor, quite a bit more.

INFANTICIDE. EPIDEMIC ON THE 'QT'. All too often, when the handicapped are deemed *'too inconvenient'* for caregivers to mange they are *'put down'.* The Chinese use the term, *'euthanized'*, but the end it's the same. *It means that the precious light of a human life has been extinguished.*

The handicapped who are tucked away in institutions or at home are the lucky ones. Just as often, they are *'disposed of'* in hospital if the problem is obvious at birth.

BLESSINGS TO US ALL. While it makes many people uncomfortable to look upon or deal with the handicapped, it's to our benefit that we do. In a civilized nation we look upon the handicapped as our 'teachers' and 'role models' for compassion and caring.

The handicapped and infirm comprise a valuable element of Western Society. Their presence among us makes us a better, more compassionate, kinder, and more civilized people. Of course, who ever said the Han Chinese were 'civilized?'

'K.I.D.' KILLED IN DELIVERY. Many of the little ones are simply put to death in the very hospitals in which they are born. The birth record is often never created. Whether as a matter of sexual preference or for the simple *'convenience'* of not having a child, babies are often killed on delivery.

No birth record means the birthing couple can avoid the mountains of paperwork, red tape, and exorbitant fees necessary to gain permission for a chance at another child.

This *'hurdle'* is overcome with either a clerical *'oopsie'* or an overt, *"Give me three thousand yuan [about five-hundred United States dollars] and this never happened."* **The horror of infanticide in China is epidemic.**

'KILL IT BEFORE IT CRIES'. I can remember during my time in emergency wards, maternity wards, and on general hospital duties, witnessing many disturbing practices. Disturbing as so many practices are, nothing prepared me for the cold-blooded murder of partial and fully born children.

In one scenario I relate from my experience in a maternity hospital. We were delivering a child prematurely. The baby was about seven months along [a gestation period of 7 months [barring complications] means the baby is usually able to survive birth with minimal maintenance and medical intervention.]

However, there had been complications including severe bleeding so we decided that a 'C-Section' was in order. We delivered the baby. I noticed immediately that this was not 'a' baby, but two babies, a set of conjoined [Siamese] twins.

They were moderately physically joined at mid torso. Other than this, the children were alive and viable. While a major deformity, the surgery for separating such a set of twins is often relatively straight forward and readily available.

The delivering surgeon handed me the babies and I began to clean them up. As I was working on the kids another doctor snatched them from my hands saying, "You are obviously new here."

As he spoke, this 'doctor' severed one of the baby's heads with a large pair of scissors and tossed the children into the waste bin at the foot of the table. I just stood there, shocked, and didn't know what to say.

I have seen my share of horror stories in this area and will not go into further detail.

Note. *Unauthorized births are those where the family has failed to secure permission from government to have the child. This is most common in 'second-child' births where the children are often destroyed immediately upon delivery.

'BIRTH NAZIS'. **ABORTION STORM TROOPERS.** *'Full-term Abortion'* is rampant in many cities where birth police are particularly vigilant. The size of the city has nothing to do with the vigilance of these *'Birth Nazis'* as they often work on a *'bonus per baby'* basis and can garner an excellent income with a little hard work.

Tales abound where women, full-term and often only a few weeks or even days from their official *'due date'* are snatched off the streets or from their workplaces and taken to a hospital for the deadly procedure of *'Full-term Abortion'*.

Without medication for the mother these babies are ripped from their mothers' wombs and murdered on the spot. All too often, hospital staff allow a few minutes of life laying the child on its mother's chest. Here it will lay only long enough for her to see it before they kill the child and toss it in the trash.

More and more often hospital administrators are demanding payment for this murderous service.

The cost of having your baby ripped from your womb and murdered is usually around three thousand yuan [*about five-hundred United States Dollars*]. Some mothers, unable to pay, end up in debtor's prisons. Yes, China has debtor's prisons. *More on that later.*

WE DON'T SERVE *'YOUR KIND'*. When you walk into a fast food restaurant, even one of those famous American chain stores, in China the first thing to strike your attention is that the order counter is almost always on the second floor and hence, inaccessible to the handicapped.

The restrooms are also on the second floor [*if there are restrooms at all*] and they too are almost never '*handicapped accessible*'. A Chinese *'squat toilet'* requires levels of fitness, dexterity, flexibility, and stamina so often not possessed by the elderly, infirm, or obese. There are no lifts or escalators. There are certainly no wheelchair ramps.

I DO NOT BELIEVE IN COINCIDENCE!

ENGINEERED INACCESSIBILITY. As a man of science I don't believe in coincidence. All things happen for a reason. The reason for isolated order counters and bathrooms is obvious. China's *'society'* at large is so unwilling to tolerate the infirm among them that they engineer this isolation into their very architecture in order to *'keep the cripples out'*.

There's no way in Hell its just a *'coincidence'* when it happens again and again. As a matter of fact, second-floor bathrooms and order counters are established elements of commercial retail architecture in China.

JUST A SIDE NOTE. When you finally find a restroom, there will most certainly be no hot water or toilet paper. Not missing are the unavoidable aromas that only a well-used latrine can provide. Oh the smells of China!

I have a good friend who is afflicted with severe Rheumatoid Arthritis [*R.A.*] and, as with all R.A. sufferers; she has her *good* days and her *bad* days. On a *'bad'* day, she cannot eat at any of these fast-food chains as they offer no way for her to even get into the store.

Even more traditional *'sit down'* restaurants (*where waiters and waitresses serve you*) are generally inaccessible to the handicapped, lacking wheelchair ramps or even a hand rail on the stairs. Beyond being handicap inaccessible is the often overt refusal to serve the handicapped.

One day I went with friends to a major burger franchise, one of America's top two. As two of us lifted our colleague's wheelchair into the store (*it actually had a first floor service counter*) we, along with our wheelchair-bound friend, were physically pushed out the door.

What the restaurant workers had to say I have heard before. *"We don't serve 'their kind' in here."*

Feeling much like a black man in South Africa during the 1970's, I waited outside with my friend in her wheelchair while our other companion went inside and bought our meals. We had decided that, as it was a nice day [*in Beijing a nice day is any day you can see the sky*] we would eat outside.

We sat at clean umbrella-equipped tables which littered the sidewalk outside the restaurant. I moved a chair aside, my handicapped friend pulled up into position at the table, and our third colleague arrived heavily laden with our soon-to-be-consumed victuals.

It was only moments later that we were hassled by a walking policeman [*possibly private security, in China they all look alike*] who told us that we could not *'park'* the wheelchair in a public place. We had to move on.

DEPARTMENT STORES AND MALLS. Chinese cities often have really new and modern retail facilities with every kind of shop imaginable. One can buy pretty much anything here from Italian suits and leather goods to gourmet ice cream. These newly built and beautifully designed shopping malls and gallerias offer truly world-class shopping.

Abounding are gleaming glass and metal multi-story buildings with every possible convenience available from decorative water fountains to ice skating rinks. But handicapped access is almost never to be had.

These newly designed glass and metal edifices sport incredibly long escalators gleaming in the light which filters through the overhead skylight ceilings. Off in the corner, hidden behind a fire hose station, one might see the doors of a lift, an elevator.

But wait! On closer inspection, these lifts are, more often than not, *'for service workers only'* and are usually kept locked.

If the lifts are not locked they are so small as to accommodate only two or three people of *'average size'.* If it's open to the public the line is sure to be *"longer than a homemade prayer."*

These elevators, it seems, are only used when large items that are too heavy for stairs or too wide for the escalators have to be moved. They are not intended for human occupation.

Some of these malls, the really huge ones, boast the *'sky ride'* design of elevator. You can see these glass capsules sliding up and down through a clear glass tube carrying happy shoppers from floor to floor on their various expeditions of retail expenditure.

Unfortunately, these are always over-used and never large enough to fit more than say, two to four standing people or two people in wheelchairs. Were you to attempt to take this lift in your wheelchair or with a walker, either you would wait upwards of ten minutes for your turn, or you would be sent away by mall security.

"Well," you think, *"That's okay. There's still the escalator."*

Again, **NOT HAPPENING.** *The escalators spend more time off than on* in order to save money on electricity and maintenance. Besides, *escalators and wheelchairs don't mix!*

MAINTAINING ESCELATORS AND LIFTS. My brief investigation found only a few *certified* firms in all of Beijing [a city of eighteen million people] licensed to service escalators. These maintenance firms have very few techs on staff. The result is that these firms charge outrageous fees and put customers on a 'waiting list' as they are the only acts in town. *Aah, the joys of a monopoly.*

Business and mall managers, among others, wish to avoid the problems and expense of escalator maintenance by simply turning them off. Sometimes, and this is interesting, they will turn on only the *'up'* escalator but leave the *'down'* one off or vice versa. This *'selective use of escalators'* serves two purposes:

- It saves on *'wear and tear'*, inevitably lowering maintenance costs on expensive escalators.

- It *'herds'* customers on various floors giving them more incentive to shop a little more because the way down is not an easy one. Truly advanced crowd control is possible with the judicious use of escalators by turning them on and off at the right times of day.

THEY CAN MAKE IT BUT THEY CAN'T FIX IT. It seems that with a people capable of copying or building virtually anything from bubble gum machines to spacecraft, nobody knows how to fix these things when they break. One such *'difficult-to-impossible-to-fix'* thing seems to be the escalator.

Behold the roots of the greatest *'throw away'* society in the world. These people don't just throw away their broken toys which are often easily repairable. They throw away their people as well.

PRISONERS OF THE MALL. I once witnessed an elderly couple who had gone shopping on the fourth floor of a major department store.

When it came time to leave they found themselves trapped as, when they had taken the *'up'* escalator, they had failed to notice that the *'down'* escalator had been turned off.

Unable to descend the *'down'* escalator manually (*due to old age and infirmity*) they waited in the store for over two hours until management finally relented and turned on the *'down'* escalator only long enough to get these *'troublemakers'* out of the store. Once the older couple had left, management turned the escalator back off.

If you've ever climbed or descended an escalator that is out of service, you know that any number of floors can become an impossible obstacle even for a healthy and reasonably fit person. *There is something about the pitch or spacing of an escalator stair that makes it much tougher going than an ordinary staircase.*

"WHERE OH WHERE CAN IT BE?" I remember taking my shiny new car to the dealership for service and watching in suppressed amusement as five service technicians tried in vain to locate the spare tire:

It was a bright, sunny morning as I pulled into the dealership where I had bought this beautiful 'fully loaded' and 'top of the line' Honda Cross Tour Sedan only weeks earlier. The car was a beauty and I was initially very happy with it, figuring the vehicle's few bugs would soon be worked out.

I had brought it in for a checkup prior to a long road trip I was about to take. I asked the men to check fluids, tires, filters, etc. About a half hour later I noticed a couple of technicians circling my car as though it had just hatched from a giant egg.

Obviously dumbfounded, they lifted and closed the hatchback a number of times, poked through our belongings in storage in the back, and even looked under the passenger seats. When they had finally gotten to raising the hood for a third or fourth time I decided that intervention was due.

"Problems, gentlemen?" **I proffered. "Yes,"** answered the Service Manager flanked by two technicians. *"We cannot seem to locate your spare tire. Have you removed it?"*

I said nothing and lifted the hatchback, popped up a plastic cap near the rear bumper, and inserted the handle of the tire wrench / jack handle into the hole. The handle fit neatly in the slot which was clearly labeled in English and Chinese, *"Lift panel and insert tire tool to access spare tire"*.

I spun the wrench as the service crew watched in amazement. They stood in awe as the spare tire lowered from the back of the car's underbelly.

The Service Manager and technicians turned away. They were rightfully shamed that I knew more about this car than they did. Nothing was said for the longest time. Such is the state of the art of service and maintenance in China.

Intent not to *'rub it in'* I gave these men a little while to deal with their moment of shame.

A COUNTERFEIT CAR. I was to later discover that my *'shiny beauty'* was largely fake. What do I mean by fake? A trip to a Beijing dealership revealed that this top of the line luxury car was fully equipped with aftermarket and counterfeit accessories and parts.

From the rear view camera to the very rear view mirrors themselves it seems every possible accessory item that could be replaced with knock-off aftermarket equipment had been replaced. Even the automatic transmission was not original equipment!

Simply put, this car was a pile of *'knocked-off'* aftermarket junk and parts squeezed and pinched into the semblance of a Honda Luxury Car. When purchased I had been assured that all accessories were original equipment assembled with the car in the Honda factory.

This does, in part, explain why nobody seemed able to fix the many little bugs and glitches in the system. It took legal action and a great deal of patience to recover my financial losses.

Note. In China's headlong rush to college educate all their young they have lost almost all their skilled tradesmen. They do, however, have a good supply of well-trained civil attorneys who know every loophole and 'back-door' in the hugely flawed Chinese legal system.

THE TALE OF ANOTHER SHINY NEW CAR. I went to a major Honda Automobile Dealer and saw no less than two dozen nearly-new late-model cars sitting under tarpaulins in an open lot behind the office.

There they sat because nobody could figure out what was wrong with them. I learned these cars had been there several months and were due to be loaded up and taken to Shanghai for reconditioning and resale.

Yet another experience of mine showed the five-man staff of this car dealership was inept at best. Between five men they were unable to even test my car's electrical system.

When I looked in their service bay I noticed all manner of diagnostic equipment, computers and shiny roll-away tool boxes everywhere in this *'Class A'* shop. They were beautiful, advanced, and largely unused.

The computers and high tech diagnostic equipment, all less than five years old, sat under dusty plastic covers having never been used.

At the core of this visit was the fact that my car battery would lose all its power overnight. I needed a 'jump start' every day. This only happened in the cold weather. They were unable to figure this out and kept swapping out the battery.

Five batteries in only a week ought to have told these morons something!

By *'trading-in'* my car on a newer one I got out of this mess.

CHAPTER 3

PUBLIC TRANSPORTATION FOR THE HANDICAPPED

BUS DRIVERS SAY *"NO"*. Well, here's another great chance to see something you don't want to try if you are at all handicapped. Try taking the bus.

Beijing buses are new, sleek, pretty, and totally ill-equipped for the handicapped. If a would-be rider has a walker, for example, a bus won't even stop to let him on.

If a handicapped person is in a mixed crowd [*a crowd composed of both handicapped and non-handicapped people*] waiting at the bus stop, the bus will stop but the driver will wave off anyone appearing to be handicapped.

If challenged the driver has an excuse committed to memory. *"I'm not going to be responsible for you."* or *"I'm not equipped to carry your kind."* Parroting memorized response is something the Chinese excel at.

SHAMELESS ROBBERS AND LIARS. With a job as taxi driver only a bribe or two away, and with no moral compass, taxi drivers are by and large (*with few exceptions*) thieves and scoundrels of the lowest order.

When a blind person hails a cab the driver considers him to be *'easy money'*. It's only too easy to make more money by driving the blind person around just a little more, taking *'the scenic route'* or simply misquoting the amount shown on the meter.

Life for the blind in a Chinese taxi can be expensive and dangerous.

I once donned dark glasses and borrowed a white cane from a colleague. I then took three cab rides through the city to various destinations and was, surely enough, ripped off on each and every trip.

Being of Asian descent and speaking Chinese very well, I was never spotted as a foreigner. This is important as cabbies make a regular practice of cheating foreigners.

Trips which should have cost around twelve yuan ended up costing nearly twenty. One cabby, who *'helped me sort through my change'* took a one-hundred yuan note from my hand.

After taking the hundred yuan note he still insisted on the overcharge of twenty yuan for the trip!

SUBWAY TRAINS. These are an efficient way to get from here to there as long as you aren't handicapped. The Chinese government, much to its credit, has done much to improve and expand this method of public transportation.

Unfortunately, again there seem to be no plans for making it accessible to the handicapped.

I can remember descending over 120 stairs (*on an escalator which was, of course, shut off at the time*) to get into a subway station. Once within the belly of the subway beast one finds getting onto the train an ordeal at best and an absolute impossibility at worst.

Note. Think 'Japanese Subways' and remove any possible semblance of order or organization. Now you have a picture of the pandemonium that is the Chinese Subway System.

Whether sighted and physically fit or blind and physically challenged, the real trick is to ride the great leviathan. The biggest part of this challenge is the Chinese people themselves. In China people *WILL NOT* help you or offer you a seat.

They won't even hold a door for you. The fact is, if you are obviously physically challenged, people will deliberately shove you out the door and back onto the platform.

"IT'S NOT MY BUSINESS." The Chinese mantra, "*It's not my business*", coupled with a lack of anything even partially resembling compassion or morality, has helped the Chinese people to rank among the most socially worthless and self-centered people on the planet.

TO SUM IT UP: If you are handicapped and want to go anywhere in China, be sure and bring a sighted companion with you. I don't care how *'independent'* you are.

These bastards are cunning and conniving and you won't stand a chance against them in *'their'* world. If you are a woman, don't even *dream* of it!

CHAPTER 4

'TO SERVE AND PROTECT'

POLICE AND HOSPITALS IN CHINA

"IT'S NOT MY BUSINESS." I once witnessed an elderly woman being accosted by two young men on the street not fifty feet from a police station.

A great crowd of gawkers had assembled but nobody was willing to do anything to assist the old dear.

The errant teens were pushing her back and forth as she fought to keep her balance and her purse. These shining examples of Chinese youth acted as though they were immune to any intervention. Normally, in China, that would have been true, but not this time.

Being afflicted with *'western chivalry'* and compassion, I stepped in and subdued one of her attackers with a swinging left cross to the head. He fell like a sack of rice on a loading dock and didn't move.

Turning to the other miscreant I advanced on him only a few steps and he jumped like a jack rabbit. The craven teen ran through the crowd like Hell was on his trail as he bumped into people and even the corner of building in his efforts to get away from me.

As a reward for my actions I found myself detained by the police. These were the very same cops who, only moments earlier, had been hiding behind the doors of the police office.

These cowardly *'boys-in-blue'* only emerged from their safe place when I had done their work for them. I was held and repeatedly questioned and threatened for three hours as *'an accomplice'* to the crime.

Police and authorities could not understand why I chose to intervene. ***Welcome to China!*** Chivalry and courage are ever absent behind the Bamboo Curtain. Compassion in China is rarer than the largest gemstone.

I suspect it was the fact that I made the police *'lose face'*, and look bad in the eyes of the dozens of onlookers that prompted them to arrest me. Indeed, onlookers cheered me and jeered at the police with shouts of, *"Where were you!"* and *"Why did a citizen have to do your job?"* all the while not considering their own lack of involvement.

I retained a pretty good lawyer who had me freed that evening with a warning and a small fine. In all, his fees and the fine came to five-hundred fifty yuan [*about ninety United States Dollars*].

I was also informed in no uncertain terms that saving a life or helping the helpless are not tolerated in China and that in so doing I might well open myself to criminal prosecution.

The results of practicing chivalry on any scale could well culminate in my deportation or even incarceration. The laws are so written as to discourage anyone in this land where life is cheap from helping anyone else in anything other than a casual setting.

HOSPITALS. Get ready for this! Even the newest hospitals in China, if they are only three or four floors high, **often have no lifts or escalators.** It's not uncommon to see family members carrying the ill *'piggy-back-style'* up the stairs as many hospitals don't even have orderlies. In China, hospitals rely on family to carry or wheel patients around as needed.

These hospitals have top-notch surgical staff by any world standards! Their doctors are sharp, well trained, and caring by and large.

The surgical suites are like something out of Star Trek and the people know how to use all that shiny stuff to accomplish a surgical success rate that makes Britain, Canada, and even United States medicine blush in shame!

BUT JUST TRY TO FIND A WHEELCHAIR! This hospital owns about twenty wheelchairs according to records.

Most of them are either broken or stolen. Yes, City-living Han Chinese will, by and large, will steal anything not firmly nailed down, set in cement, or bolted to a nearby building and kept under guard.

B.Y.O.W. *Bring your own Wheelchair* ... and lock it to the bed. Lacking a moral compass, the Chinese have developed some rather disturbing habits.

I was watching a doctor consult a patient in a hallway. As he finished his cigarette he crushed it out on the floor with his shoe.

He then called a nurse to help get the elderly man to an examining room. Smoking by staff and patients alike is common in most Chinese hospitals.

IN BROAD DAYLIGHT. As the nurse arrived and began to chat with the man I noticed a young fellow kneeling beside the elderly patient's bed. The youngster's hands worked deftly and with great precision.

Moments later he was casually wheeling the wheelchair which had sat beside the bed, previously locked to the radiator on the wall, toward the front doors of the hospital lobby.

So smooth was his appropriation of this wheelchair that I thought it was his. His work was as quick and trouble-free as though he had simply unlocked the padlock, rolled up the chain, and gone his merry way.

As the thief disappeared into the crowd it was then that I noticed the padlock, shackle still secure, fastened to a freshly-cut length of chain on the floor where the wheelchair had once been.

Oh well, even if I had known and intervened, I might well have risked deportation or something even worse. Welcome to China!

CHAPTER 5
'GOING PLACES' & 'BEING PLACES'

To QUEUE OR NOT TO QUEQUE. Lining up, simply form-ing a line, is something that is virtually *'automatic'* to pretty much everyone I know in England or America. When you go to see a film, buy groceries, seek services at the bank, or simply need to *'take a turn'*, a queue is usually what naturally occurs.

Not in China! It seems that the Chinese almost universally feel an indescribable drive, an unquenchable thirst to be *'first-in-line'* no matter what the venue. It would almost seem this is hard-wired into their DNA.

Whether in a fast-food restaurant or a bank it just kills the Chinese to be *'behind'* anyone. This is a tendency which carries over onto the highways and byways with those Chinese who drive, *but more on that later.*

Only in the last five or six years have I seen banks and govern-ment offices adopt the *'Take-A-Number'* system. This has been a boon to banking and retail businesses in China.

I admit that it can be quite entertaining to sit back and watch them as they scurry about and slam into one another in their *'quest for first place'*.

Like debris in a tornado they collide and crash in into each other in a kaleidoscopic array of chaos as each seeks his *place* in their race to nowhere.

However, getting caught up in the maelstrom yourself isn't nearly as entertaining. It can, in fact, be extremely frustrating at best and maddening at worst. One more directionless piece of shrapnel in this destructive whirlwind of undisciplined humanity doesn't matter to them, but it can be hell to a civilized man.

Note. In our society there are two prevailing descriptions of Hell. There's the Dantean vision of flames and eternal torment, and then there's queuing up in China.

Even today as I wait to get a ticket for the train, or in line at the bank, even with the Take-A-Number system and well fenced off line barriers, the *'line-jumpers'* continue in their quest to be *'in first place'*.

By and large, the City Han Chinese <u>are</u> a silly little people. Come now, let's not pull our punches. But for those few exceptions to whom this book is dedicated, these are a remarkably stupid people.

Their complete inability to cooperate with or learn from others or from their own mistakes makes me crazy! Even my pet Labrador

Retriever learns once he has been hit in the nose with a newspaper two or three times! If these people were dogs, they would be deemed *'Un-trainables'*. However, being people, I refer to them as *'The Un-teachables.'*

Note. I have found that from classroom situations to life itself, the Chinese People have a difficult, if not impossible, time in learning from the mistakes of others.

CHAOS IN THE SHADOW OF THE BAMBOO CURTAIN. One need only walk about any city or town to notice that the people of China are remarkably oblivious to the presence of each another.

Their complete absence of discipline, organization, and common sense is obvious as they walk along the footpaths and in the streets. Even on casual observation one immediately notices that they are literally bumping into each other all the way up and down the street.

Like flies in a bad restaurant or seagulls at a landfill, this is not *'traffic'* but rather a completely undisciplined mass of Chinese humanity in an almost aimless wandering. The recent proliferation of mobile phones in China has only served to exacerbate the situation. *More on that later.*

SHENYANG ROULETTE. Crossing the street in China is an adventure and indeed a very interesting study in a uniquely Chinese brand of stupidity and incivility. I can safely say that only a very small percentage of Chinese people actually use the crosswalks. It is to them I dedicate this book.

Climbing safety barriers and squeezing between cars, trucks, and buses which are momentarily stalled in traffic is an all-too-frequent behavior of the Chinese pedestrian. I have come to call this unique behavior, *'Shenyang Roulette'*. Hundreds of people are killed every year practicing this *'sport'*.

Despite the fact that the law requires that motorists yield right of way to pedestrians in crosswalks, it almost never happens. Motorists either don't care, or they don't know.

Standing near any busy intersection for any length of time will almost assuredly demonstrate to you a plethora of events in which cars and people have close calls or outright collisions.

Cars, bicycles, motorbikes, trucks, and all manner of vehicles and pedestrians are all equally at fault in this mass of utter confusion on the street corners of China.

MORE ON SHENYANG ROULETTE.   It's impossible to guess what's going on in the feeble minds of these little people as they *'play the game'* of Shenyang Roulette.

Dashing across multiple lanes of moving traffic and squeezing between the bars of the safety fences, they continue to dash across impossibly busy lanes of traffic. People getting *'clipped'* by cars is a common event resulting in the pedestrian getting up, swearing at the driver, and running off.

Equally amusing is to watch how those in cars, determined to neither slow down or stop in their mission to *'get somewhere first'* literally brush pedestrians out of the way without a second thought.

Using their car bumpers as *'brooms'* motorists will literally push people out of the way because it's both unfathomable and inexcusable to them that they should have to slow or [*perish the thought*] stop for something as insignificant as another human being.

Be sure as you walk across the street, even in a crosswalk, even with the *'Walk'* light in your favor, <u>that</u> car <u>is</u> going through, and you'd best understand that its driver *WILL* run you over if you want to press the issue.

CHAPTER 6

THE 'INS & OUTS' OF CHINA

ELEVATORS, ESCALATORS,

& REVOLVING DOORS

AN ABSENCE OF ELEVATOR ETTIQUETTE. As lifts become more common in China, we see immediately that the Chinese are not yet ready for this mechanical innovation. They seem both confused and frustrated by these modern contrivances.

The Chinese People's innate inability to learn through experience or by watching others is never more evident than when watching a lift in operation.

When a lift arrives, for example, on the ground floor, it's often loaded with passengers eager to egress this box en route to their daily tasks. In China this means, *'Let the games begin.'*

Those Chinese who have been waiting for the elevator car's arrival now push their way in with a completely unexplainable madness.

The tide of mentally deficient, self-centered people then streams into the elevator car. The mad inrush of humanity works hard to prevent anyone still inside from ever getting out.

This shove-fest continues until one side overpowers the other and something happens.

Han-Jams. Whether it's an overcrowded elevator car with a whining overload alarm, or there are so many people that the doors can't close, we now have the human equivalent of a log-jam. I call these 'Han-Jams'.

Note. I have seen such events take upward of ten minutes to clear as people lose patience and eventually filter out of the elevator car, heading for the nearest stairwell. Aah, stairwells ... more on those later.

In the west, where the lift was not only invented, but proliferates in nearly every corner of residence and business, we have developed what I call *"Elevator Etiquette"*.

It's this etiquette which has made these contraptions not only readily understandable, but commonplace and convenient.

THE RULES OF ELEVATOR ETTIQUETTE.

Rule 1. First in, last out. When one enters a lift, he should proceed to the back of the cabinet so as to allow others to enter and find a place. When the lift arrives, people should leave in turn, making no great press on others as they do so.

At most, a hand's touch on the shoulder to separate the folks in front of you, accompanied by a polite, *"Excuse me, please."* generally gets the job done.

Rule 2. Empty the lift before filling it. When a lift arrives on the ground floor and one is waiting for it, one should wait until the lift has completely emptied of its current riders before entering.

Rule 3. Women, Children, Elderly, and Infirm First. This speaks for itself to the modern man but may require clarification in some areas of the world.

It simply means that a common exercise of chivalry in allowing those less able than one's self to enter or leave a lift first is socially required.

It's maddening to ride a lift in China. I have occasionally had to physically knock people down to escape the lift. If you don't push and shove your way out, you're often in for *'the scenic route'* on this elevator car. If you're unwilling to push them down to get out I hope you packed a lunch!

I have found myself smothered by the inrush of some thirty people or more trying to occupy the already half-full elevator cabinet.

As I have said before, I am a man of considerable stature, and if this is overwhelming to me, imagine how it must be to someone about five feet in height weighing perhaps 100 pounds. They fall victims to the *'Han Herd.'*

'SELF-CLEANING STAIRS'. Known to most of us as escalators, these are really interesting. *Most of the time escalators are turned* *off.* If you come across an escalator that is on and running: *Let the games begin!* In the west, I could make a sporting event out of watching and betting on Chinese escalator traffic!

I spend uncountable moments every week watching people plug up the entrances and exits of these automatic stairs in their typically uncontrollable swarm.

They stand in that narrowest of all places where people exit the electric stairs and chat, smoke, adjust their clothing, tie their shoes, answer the phone, and so on.

They do all this with no idea or concern that it might be making things difficult for others. They stand there, oblivious to the impending onslaught.

Unlike an elevator, an escalator has the great benefit that it will eject the idiots who don't know it's time to get off. For this reason I call them, *"Self-cleaning Stairs."*

Like a NASCAR auto race, I watch for the crashes. I tell my wife I'm just *'people watching'* which I do a great deal of. This is only a half-truth as I'm really waiting to see just how many people it takes to crash through the *'people barrier'*, the *'Great Wall of Chinese'* at the top of the escalator.

OF STAIRS AND STAIRWELLS. Often I find myself wending my way up a deactivated escalator or stairwell.

The forty or so stairs take a good five minutes to ascend as I step over and around people. It's like walking through a minefield.

Occasionally I must actually physically move people who are sitting, reading, chatting on the phone, meeting with others, etc.

For some reason it seems that the word, **"*stairwell*"** has become synonymous with **"*gathering place*"** to the Chinese.

These stairs are not *'self-cleaning'*. In China, a land where stairwells abound and lifts do not; this is a sad commentary on a silly people.

DOORWAYS. Despite the *'PUSH'* and *'PULL'* signs being written in Chinese on doors, many people can be seen tugging or pushing when they should be pushing or tugging.

In the West, this is the material of comedy skits on late night television or a clown's bit in the center ring of a circus. But in China it's just another part of everyday life. The fact that the door doesn't move when they push against it does nothing to signal to these folks that, perhaps, a pull or tug on that door handle just might do the job.

I have watched a half dozen people pile up at a restaurant door before an employee is finally sent to open that door for them. These ignorant customers then begin to complain about *'locked doors'* when it's more a case of *'locked brains.'*

I have seen folks injured as they put their hands or elbows through the door's glass while trying to push it open. Despite the price of new glass *'every month or so'*, a restaurant I know of refuses to replace glass with wood or metal. I have also learned that they actually keep a *'spare window'* in the back room.

ROUND AND ROUND SHE GOES. These are another matter and are closely watched by employees of hotels and buildings which have those rotating contraptions known as *'revolving doors'*. It turns out that revolving door injuries are frequent and occasionally quite severe.

According to China Fire Services, revolving door accidents occur so regularly as to have their own response code. People just wander into the glass, get *'caught up'* in the revolving door, and then shit happens!

I have seen people who have gotten their arms, fingers, hands, legs, neckties, skirts and dresses, shoe laces, and belts caught up. Such a sight to see!

Always these incidents occur in some really original or *'new'* way and the unique elements of each happening provide a rich source of entertainment for the callous and slightly sadistic observer such as myself.

I can still remember one guy who managed to get his arm stuck in the revolving door in a backward *'hammer lock'* which put him in great pain, dislocating his elbow.

The result was that Fire Services had to be called in. Those brave young men of the fire department ended up removing the door from its mount. Their labors resulted in freedom for this hapless miscreant, no longer trapped in the glass and steel jaws of the revolving leviathan.

I recollect the day the brave young men of the local fire company came out to rescue a man trapped in the teeth of the monster revolving door at a local hotel.

A STORY WORTH RECOUNTING:

The sun shone brightly on a Sunday afternoon as a mass of out-of-towners attending a Mah Jong tournament was swarming through the front revolving doors of the hotel. Whether going in or out one could not tell.

Such was the density and fury of this storm of Oriental Humanity as it gushed its way through the rotating vanes of the revolving door. Like water through a pump they gushed through.

Suddenly I heard a screeching noise and then saw a young man in his thirties, well-dressed, on his knees in pain.

He cried and his eyes were filled with tears. This poor man was in obvious agony. He was on one knee and his right arm was bent backward, as though by some mindless thug demanding re-payment of a debt.

As the revolving door sucked him further into jaws he was the victim of an almost perfect hammerlock. His left knee was twisted with the full weight of his body resting on it.

This poor man was completely unable to use his captured arm to alleviate the pain. This guy was screwed!

Men and women scrambled over one another climbing over each other's bodies, until only moments later the sole occupant of this disaster scene was the unlucky morsel, this tit-bit snack for the hungry revolving monster that now had him in its grip.

Hotel workers in traditional blue jumpsuits rushed to the scene but did more head-scratching than anything else. This was a job for the professionals! Someone called *'119'* which is Fire Emergency in China.

Moments later a huge well-stocked and highly populated shiny red fire engine pulled up flanked by two paramedic scooters and a squad car carrying the local engine chief.

The men dropped off the sides of the engine, came pouring out of the car, and quickly sprinted from their motorcycles. Like a well-oiled machine each man ran to his appointed station.

Working with power equipment I cannot identify even now, and obvious skill, they soon managed to lift the door out from its frame.

The door came away and a doctor who had been dispatched from the local hospital took charge. The *'victim'* was whisked away in an ambulance [*in China that's a panel van with a stretcher inside and two to four blue lights on top*]

The poor firemen were obviously doing all they could *'not to laugh'* at this stupidity, but were not completely successful. Me too.

A KIND WORD ABOUT THE BRAVE YOUNG MEN OF CHINA FIRE SERVICES: These are the very fruit of the vine, the shining examples of fine young men the Chinese people are capable of producing, but for many reasons usually do not. A more dedicated, quick-thinking, compassionate and brave group you will never meet.

WORD ON THE HOTEL. The hotel went through an experimental period replacing the door's glass panes with wooden ones. The idea was that these pretty wooden panels could be easily removed by maintenance personnel when necessary and there would be no risk of glass fragmentation injury.

The result was an alarming increase in broken noses, people being knocked down, etc. because they were entering the door *'blind'*. The revolving door has since been replaced with a high quality sliding glass door.

Every day revolving [man-eating] doors in China catch unwary and ignorant people in their jaws and inflict pain and injury. When will the madness stop! Oh, the humanity!

CHAPTER 7

DINNER, MOBILE PHONES, & TABLE MANNERS

'DINNER WITH THE HAN'

LIKE NAILING TOFU TO A TREE. Holding a conversation with Chinese is like nailing tofu to a tree. It's just not happening. These uncultured and totally self-centered people have managed to achieve levels of conversational rudeness unimaginable in the West.

This has become even more prevalent with the advent of the mobile telephone. The mobile or *'cell'* phone has infected their society with its presence and proliferation. Indeed, to date, the number of mobile phones in use in China outnumbers the combined numbers Europe and America.

From a causal dinner conversation to a formal discussion, or even simple chit-chat, the Chinese have adopted the mobile phone as yet another instrument for ratcheting their already formidable levels of rudeness to stratospheric levels.

MOBILE PHONES. In China nearly everyone has a mobile phone these days. I have seen the viral infection of digital communication as it has spread unchecked. Like a virus it runs pandemic among the people giving them even more excuses and newer ways to be rude.

AT DINNER. Imagine sitting at dinner with a half dozen friends. Laid on the table are all their mobile phones. These digital status symbols are set to 'loud' and stand ready.

They are the status symbols of a new generation. Blackberry, iPhone, HTC, whichever costs most is often *'the winner'* in this undeclared competition for status and the idiotic drive for perceived importance.

LOUD IS GOOD? Chinese being the noisiest people in the world, the volume levels of their phones can at first be a shock to the uninitiated. I have even seen people drop a drink or spill food when one of these noise-makers kicks in during dinner.

As for those set on *'vibrate'*, forget it being any less annoying! I have never seen more active and formidable vibration in such a small appliance. These phones seem equally suited for Swedish Massage as for notifying someone of an incoming call or message.

When that phone goes off you can see the wine in a glass across the table ripple! As some conversation begins to develop one notices that everyone is carefully eyeing their phones, in the expectation or hope that it will soon ring.

Everyone is praying for the chance to show their importance by *'getting a call on the cell'*. Then, like a slave at the beck and call of his master, someone's phone rings and in a flash that phone is on the owner's ear.

"*Wei?*" is the immediate response from the dinner guest. Mid-sentence and mid-conversation, he has dumped you for his digital master's summons. As the Chinese are a very loud-voiced and noisy people, the phone conversation immediately drowns out all other conversation in the room.

Yes, even louder than the cacophony of whistles and bells of the ringing phones, is the almost comically loud voice of its owner.

Others, being of the same ilk, simply stop talking and eat, light up a cigarette, or just lean back in their chairs and do nothing. Just as often, however, this is all the excuse the others need to dial someone up almost as if to see who can show the least civility.

They then embark on one of the many "*talk-a-thons*" which generally signal the premature end of what was to have been a social dinner.

I have actually seen a Chinese man giving a toast to a guest at a large dinner in a nice restaurant quit mid-sentence as he answers that phone which has so loudly screamed, "*Answer Me.*"

Others at the table simply watched, and then broke into other conversations as this now telephone-bound person at least took the time to leave the table and carry his conversation to the other side of the room.

Of course, being Chinese means being very loud. This man's entire conversation was still easily heard across the room and even in the outer hallway where I had run to get away.

I had run here in a vain attempt to retreat from the verbal pandemonium.

Knowing the Chinese as well as I do, this was more for his own convenience than that of his companions and guests.

Within ten minutes, nearly everyone was on the phone and the din had become such that I had to leave the room just to hear myself think. This went on for nearly twenty minutes. I went home. *Nobody noticed.*

'ON CALL 24/7.' The mobile phone has so spread in commonality and perceived importance that people are quite *'put out'* if you aren't available twenty four hours a day. Yes, they actually 'expect' that phone to be on and at your side at all times.

Now, I am neither a surgeon *'on-call'* nor am I an important government official awaiting news of some political crisis. Therefore my phone gets turned off at night.

People hear this and they are shocked! Some are so utterly surprised that they refuse to believe I actually shut my phone off at night. It draws the same incredulous response as when I tell them that I don't watch television!

Personally, a good night's sleep is worth missing some *'emergency'* whatever it may be perceived to be. I have a fire alarm if my house catches fire and a *'land line'* phone if there is a real emergency. What else does anyone really need? think 1970s.

TABLE MANNERS IN CHINA. *There are no table manners in China.* If the table is small enough, people will reach in front of you, speak with mouths full of food and chomp their meals with all the grace and volume of hungry pigs at the trough. The sounds of them eating can be nearly as loud as them talking!

Chinese shout back and forth across the table with a volume level suggesting they are at a football game or an auto race.

'LIGHTING UP.' This is automatic and no consideration is given. The smoker (*more than half of Chinese adult males smoke according to the National Ministry of Health's report in 2014*) will then light up, puff smoke at you from across the table and, once finished, crush out his cigarette in his food or yours.

CUT OFF AT THE TABLE. Anywhere, at any time, be prepared to be cut off mid-sentence on an irritatingly regular basis. With or without a mobile phone at their disposal, this is just *'business as usual'* to the Chinese.

Regardless of the situation, it seems a Chinese imperative to cut you off. Trust me! They'll do this <u>every</u> time!

Even if they've no incoming call or other viable reason, it will happen, so just be prepared for this extra little rudeness which the Chinese toss around with such wanton disregard.

IN THE CLASSROOM. Even as a college professor at one of China's most prestigious universities, it's a daunting task to get my students to turn off or at least silence their mobile phones during my lectures.

I have found through unfortunate experience that no amount of threat or promise can get this new generation, literally raised on mobile phones and devoid of any civility or manners, to separate themselves from their digital addiction.

Raised by inconsiderate and rude parents, descended of a rude and inconsiderate race, the fruit really doesn't fall far from the tree.

And, worst of all, there is no hope in sight because, *'mobile phone or no mobile phone'* the Chinese will continue to find new ways of being rude and inconsiderate.

It has always been this way and will always be. It's in their rearing, their culture, and probably programmed into their very DNA!

Note. I know many Chinese who, so addicted to their phones, will travel an hour by bus or train to pick up the cell phone they left at home. These people are literally 'crippled' without their 'digital masters'. No they're not doctors-on-call or emergency workers, they're just addicts.

CHAPTER 8
CHINA'S ROAD ROYALTY
AUTOMOBILES IN CHINA

MOTORING. This is perhaps the most amazing, shocking, and dangerous level of herd behavior [*or lack thereof*] anywhere in the world. The Chinese have more drive to *'get ahead of everyone else'* than lemmings marching to the sea.

Worse than crying, *"Fire"* in a crowded movie theater or setting off a bomb at a football game, the pandemonium experienced among the Chinese on the road is far greater and infinitely more frightening.

It's this press of urgency with which the Chinese have brought their silly and dangerous behavior to humanity in frightening reality. China's roads have become the battle ground for those fighting for some intangible supremacy. Their reward is always forever beyond their reach as there is always someone *'just ahead of them'*.

LET'S BEGIN WITH A FEW FACTS:

FACT 1. Over ninety percent of Chinese motorists obtain their operator permits by fraudulent means, always involving bribes and collusion. Without paying these bribes, it is literally impossible to get an operator's permit by following the rules. *This set of statistic and fact comes from the Public Safety Bureau's Department of Motor Vehicle Statistics as of March, 2015.*

FACT 2. Special Operators, such as taxi drivers, bus drivers, operators of large lorries [*trucks*], have no qualification process which is not easily circumvented with bribes and collusion. *This statistic has also been verified with the Public Safety Bureau's Department of Motor Vehicle Statistics.*

When one has obtained his license to drive by simply greasing a palm or two, one is almost universally oblivious to the laws and regulations which guide the operation of motor vehicles.

Even Chinese *'traffic police'* officers, by and large, are completely ignorant of nearly every facet of traffic law and regulation.

Having been *'given'* their driver licenses upon employment with not so much as a video to watch or a book to read, the Traffic Police hit the streets ready to enforce the rules of a system of which they are completely ignorant. Wow! Sounds like big government to me!

CASE IN POINT. I was turning right on a red light after having come to a complete stop and having looked both ways first. I signaled, pulled away from the corner, and as I pulled out into the intersection I heard someone behind me yelling. I looked in my rear view mirror and saw a policeman approaching in a *'hot-and-bothered'* state.

The cop proceeded to lecture and scold me, stating that I had just run a red light. Producing the Motor Vehicle Operator's Handbook I let him read the appropriate page.

The officer reluctantly read the page and became obviously embarrassed. Embarrassed, would make direct eye contact.

He admitted that he wasn't aware this rule. *"I'm sorry,"* he said, *"I didn't know this. Nobody told me. Is this a new law?"* I politely responded, *"Yes, fairly new."* I didn't bother to inform him that this had been law for over fifteen years since the government adopted a set of uniform traffic laws and regulations.

The man silently walked back to his assigned street corner and continued to direct traffic. Parked nearby was his police car. His car bore the white and orange identification markings of a traffic police patrol car.

How had he gotten this job? He had received no formal police training which is typical of police in China. No doubt he got his job through knowing the right people.

Once employed, he was handed a driver license on the day he was hired with no further training or testing required. He probably had *'ride-along'* training for a month or so before being sent out on his own. Welcome to China!

There is also epidemic illiteracy among Chinese police officers with nearly fifty percent being unable to read and understand the front page news on a daily newspaper. *This is according to Department of Public Safety Standards Report of 2013.*

Let's not forget one horribly disturbing fact, according to the Ministry of Education in Beijing, *"... that fewer than sixty percent of Chinese adults are functionally literate, being able to read a newspaper or magazine with clarity and reasonable understanding."*

As in most countries, a reduced I.Q. and lower level of education are fairly common among police officers. When one has obtained his driver license in the way of the Chinese, one is doomed to learn driving habits and practices by imitating those already on the road.

A COPY OF A COPY. The worst possible motoring habits are enhanced and further exacerbated (*if that is indeed possible*) as one proceeds into the world of Chinese motoring. Think of *'a copy of a copy of a copy'* and you can well understand the plethora of bad habits and dangerously stupid behavior that continues to creep into the repertoire of Chinese motorists.

Indeed, one who has absolutely no training or indoctrination to traffic laws and regulations, and is already devoid of common sense, will prove a shining example of the Chinese motorist.

BELLIGERENT. There is a certain arrogance among motorists in China, more than an arrogance, indeed it's a belligerence. Accompanying this is an unusual sense of entitlement I have never before witnessed anywhere else. In America they would get themselves shot or beaten up in short order.

I guess that's one way to weed them out. hehe. *"Send them to New York and bring back the survivors ... if there are any".*

Just watch Chinese drivers in Canada and to a lesser extent in Australia and the United States. Watch anywhere in the west where Chinese mainlanders proliferate and you'll see the same odd and dangerous behavior played out.

As the Chinese are very much a *'class-based'* society, there is a great deal of importance placed on owning and driving a car. The more expensive the car, the *'more entitled'* you are.

You are entitled to privileges and forgiveness which others are not entitled to because of your special automotive status.

It's true that Chinese who own cars are at the very least, well-to-do financially. Commoners and poor people do not drive cars as automobiles in China are among the most expensive in the world.

The great expense of cars in China is due to incredibly high sales and registration taxes imposed on all vehicles by the government in order to *'keep cars out of the hands of commoners and minorities.'*

Likewise, the cost of a driver license in China is around five hundred United States Dollars and the cost of tolls on the Chinese expressways dwarfs even that of the European Autobahn.

Between the incredibly high purchase price of a car, the astronomical cost of a driver license, and the high cost of expressway access the government has managed to ensure that only the *'most entitled'* are allowed access to automobiles.

It's interesting to note that registration and insurance costs, as well as motor fuel costs, are kept at very reasonable levels so as not to vex or annoy the powerful people who already own and drive cars in China.

Among the growing throng of motorists has emerged a new *'automotive-class-based'* society.

This class system gives rise to bizarre behavior as the royalty of the road seem to insist on having certain privileges and entitlements in recognition of their status as owners of fine automobiles.

I actually watched and listened as a motorist attempted to justify running a red light by threatening a police officer.

The driver said, *"I am driving a BMW. What does this tell you, little man?"* Immediately the officer lowered his head, cleared his throat, and apologized. He let her go on about her way.

Yes, just announcing your relationship to someone or demonstrating the size of your wallet often gets you out of trouble with the police.

The policeman's fear of this rich and powerful woman was well justified as ticketing a person with *'guanshi'* or political or personal *'connections'* necessary to afford such a car is tantamount to professional suicide ... or worse.

This woman was quite probably in a position to have had the policeman fired or punished for his impudence. How dare he ticket her! Nobody tickets a member of the road royalty!

This policeman knew that he was only a phone call away from unemployment and possibly even finding himself forever unemployable.

'CLASS' DISTINCTIONS AMONG THE ROAD ROYALTY

LOWER CLASS. Those whose cars are of a value less than *thirty-two thousand United States Dollars.* Remember that the current exchange rate is about six yuan to the dollar.

That's a chunk of change, about two hundred thousand yuan, or about three to four years income for a professional such as a school teacher or middle-management in a small company!

MIDDLE CLASS: Those whose cars are of a value between thirty *thousand and forty-eight thousand United States Dollars.*

UPPER CLASS: Those whose cars are of a value higher than forty-eight *thousand United States Dollars.*

UNTOUCHABLES: Government and Party Leaders, Taxi Drivers, Bus Drivers, Truck and Construction Equipment Operators are indeed an untouchable lot.

These people have immunity from prosecution for even the most heinous automobile-related offenses. This iron-clad protection is due to their large payments made to local police

CASE IN POINT. I drove a car which would be called "*Lower Class*", a small Honda automobile, for years.

During this time I was constantly on my guard against the indifference of taxi, bus, and truck drivers as they would frequently cut me off in traffic and box me in when parked. as though I was invisible to them.

There were numerous attempts at '*swoop and stoop**' at traffic lights. The number of ignorant or overtly malicious events perpetrated against my person was remarkably high. If you drive a cheaper car, people really are '*out to get you.*'

At police road blocks my car was always subject to scrutiny and I would be subjected to questioning in a polite but very thorough manner.

I drove a small blue Honda Civic Sedan.

---

*NOTE: "Swoop and Stoop" is when a car cuts directly in front of yours and then brakes immediately, causing you to either rear-end that car or swerve dangerously to avoid an accident.

It's extremely popular among the morons who drive taxis and is occasionally used to generate sometimes considerable revenue by the 'swooper' promising not to sue you for rear-ending him in exchange for cash at the scene.

Recently I purchased a huge black sedan, a very large SUV, a Honda Cross Tour, for around seventy-thousand United States Dollars. It's black, which signifies it possibly belongs to a government official, and it's huge, which speaks for itself, and it's obviously expensive.

Since moving up to a high-end vehicle I have noticed that the incidence of being cut off, ignored, *'swooped and stooped'*, has dropped to zero. It hasn't happened since. Such is the respect and fear all have for a car which, in their minds, quite probably carries someone important.

This car could easily be carrying a government official, a member of an official's family or a wealthy business owner.

In any case, in the mind's eye of the public, it probably has someone with sufficient connection in government to make a policeman's or *'lesser driver's'* life a living hell should there be any sort of automotive hanky-panky.

Now, when I approach road blocks, I am simply waved through (*always with a salute*). As the policeman's vision cannot penetrate my darkened windows my huge, expensive, black automobile is most intimidating.

So far advanced is the culture of *'Road Royalty'* that, were I to have an altercation with another vehicle of lesser status, the police would immediately write their report so as to favour me in all ways. After all, I have a large, beautiful, expensive luxury car. I am entitled!

Likewise, any judgments made by a traffic court would certainly be in my favour as well. So it's in China. Chairman Mao must be turning over in his grave.

LUXURY CARS IN CHINA. I spoke at length with a BMW / Audi car salesman who says that, during the six years he has sold these cars, not once has he made a private sale.

In fact, virtually every car he has ever sold has been paid for by government check or money order. He explained to me, "*Do you think someone who has worked hard to earn his money, however wealthy he might be, is going to spend this much on a car? Businessmen have a better sense of value.*"

He went on to explain that people who *earn* their money have an understanding of *'the value of a dollar'*. He reminded me that tax money is easier to come by and therefore even easier to waste in a dictatorship.

GOVERNMENT GETS ONLY THE BEST AND THAT INCLUDES CARS. One look at any government parking lot tells all. It's crowded with Honda, Toyota, Nissan, Buick, Chevy, Audi, VW, BMW automobiles, all high-end and luxury editions. There won't be a car in the lot which sells for less than forty *thousand United States Dollars.*

Those cars costing less than fifty-thousand dollars are generally *'gifts'* to faithful secretaries, wives, nieces, nephews, or good friends of the officials who pull the purse strings.

The more expensive luxury vehicles costing over fifty-thousand dollars can be assumed to be the personal cars of those officials themselves. *Ah, the glories of corruption.*

From the luxury cars to the opulent palaces where government officials *'work'*, one sees immediately that working conditions of government administrators are at the very least, opulent.

Government buildings are often lined on the outside with thin-shaved marble, sporting tall granite columns and crystal chandeliers in the lobbies.

Expensive furnishings, accessories, and services are common and are further evidence of the *'special status'* one has when working for the Communist Party, Provincial Government, or Local Government.

CHAPTER 9

MOTORCYCLES IN CHINA

AFFORDABLE TRANSPORTATION ... FOR NOW. These are a necessary means of transportation for countless millions of Chinese who simply cannot afford the punishing reality of artificially inflated high-priced automobiles.

Motorcycles generally are priced around five hundred to a thousand United States Dollars. For the people who buy these motorcycles it represents about three months' wages.

Also, the cost of a motorcycle driver license is only a fraction of the cost of a car driver license as the required bribes are smaller and the official fees are lower, those in government knowing that *"you can't get blood out of a turnip."*

IF YOU DRIVE A MOTORCYCLE. You must be wary and on your guard far more so than you would when driving in the West.

In the culture of The Road Royalty, the contempt for all things two-wheeled is obvious and even turns to an overt aggression on the part of many motorists.

This aggressive attitude of motorists toward motorcyclists has even resulted in some larger cities banning motorcycle traffic altogether. Cities such as Dalian, China have banned all motorcycle traffic in the city.

The Dalian City ban was originally enacted under the governance of Bo Xi Lai.

Bo Xi Lai [*and his wife*], for reasons other than this ban on motorcycles, has recently been arrested and is now serving a life prison sentence.

While banning motorcycles makes roads more passable for the wealthy elite who drive cars, it imposes great hardship on the poor who can only afford these two-wheeled contrivances.

Pedestrian traffic as well as bus and train ridership has increased noticeably in Dalian [*a city of seven million people*] although no new buses or trains have been added to *'take up the slack'*.

Now, I don't want to appear to exonerate motorbike operators at large because they are, by and large, even more egregious in their behavior on the road than automobile operators.

Red lights mean absolutely nothing to Chinese motorcyclists who usually have no license of any kind anyway. They trundle down the road on their cycles which are usually unregistered and are generally not even street-legal.

The use of things such as lights, brakes, or even horns is never considered as Chinese motorcyclists weave their ways through traffic, across sidewalks and safety islands, and through crosswalks.

NEVER A TRAFFIC COP WHEN YA NEED ONE. In almost all cities, there are no traffic cops at all. Save those few who populate those occasional road blocks which spring up at random locations and times, there are no traffic cops in China. Traffic police are only seen at busier and high-profile intersections.

Traffic cameras and license plate readers are relied on for all the heavy lifting in Chinese traffic enforcement. In all my years of driving in China I have never come across a moving traffic cop nor have I seen one in action.

Across China they rely on stationary traffic cameras and license plate readers almost exclusively. Being fixed-location devices this provides an 'easy out' for most drivers, especially taxi drivers.

almost comical to see a cabbie approach a freshly changed red light, turn right, go a few yards, turn a 'U' turn, come back to the same intersection and turn right again. Now he has managed to get through that red light without stopping or waiting.

This driver may have shaved as much as forty seconds off his drive time. In his insatiable drive not to stop or slow down he has saved that most precious commodity, time. It's so ridiculous as to be downright comical. Common among motorists in China is this apparent aversion to slowing or stopping for any reason.

Motorcyclists don't even bother to do this little 'turn, turn, turn' act as the traffic cameras and plate readers can't read the small tags on a motorcycle. Motorcyclists no this.

As one might expect, motorcycles suffer an inordinately high number of traffic accidents either through collision with larger vehicles or driving into the millions of unmarked open man-holes, trenches, and frost-heave canyons which litter Chinese streets. As one might expect, this adds to the overall accident and death toll considerably.

Adding insult to injury, it seems that driving a dark colored motorcycle with no lights while wearing dark colored clothing and traveling along a poorly lighted avenue is as common as a Sunday morning stroll.

The *'nighttime drive death toll'* in China is remarkably, but understandably high. This is especially true when one considers the ridiculous atmosphere surrounding such actions. I call these people *'Stealth Cyclists'*.

YES, I AM A BIKER. I ride a motorcycle for the sport and thrill of two wheels. To one uninitiated, there is no way to explain the motorcycle culture other than to say that it's more than a ride; it's a way of life.

In China, it's a dangerous adventure and you are literally flirting with death every time you hit the road. As a side note, I will **<u>NOT</u>** drive my motorcycle at night!

Unlike the locals, I wear a do-rag, helmet, glove liners, gloves, solid footwear, great eye protection, and I ride an expensive and exceptionally well-maintained Japanese-built motorcycle.

I have been a biker for decades and my pride in riding here is (*I admit more than a small degree of arrogance and prejudice*) only bolstered when I look around me. I cannot help but pity and fear the hapless, unskilled, ill-dressed masses who drive their poorly maintained motorcycles through the streets of the city.

As good a cyclist as I am, and as familiar with local roads as I am, I am still occasionally ambushed by a fresh or newly opened manholes.

There are literally thousands of open manholes in my part of the city alone, more in others.

New manholes open up daily due to poor road construction (*I have seen a manhole installed on Monday sink into the road more than a foot by Wednesday forming a potentially lethal road hazard*) or theft of the lid for its iron value.

I could regale you with unbelievable tales of my motorcycle adventures on the roads of the world's most populous country.

But I won't, as there isn't sufficient paper or time for that. Suffice it to say that driving or walking in China, whether by motorcycle or car, is like playing that nineteen-eighties video game *"Frogger."*

MORE OFFENSES TO THE SENSES
'UNTEACHABLES' ON THE ROAD'
THE SORT OF CRAP THEY GET INTO

Some of the many *'offences to the senses'* one witnesses on Chinese roads are:

EXAMPLE A. A motorist decides to let a friend into his car. So he stops in the middle of a three-lane road during rush-hour traffic and casually waits while his friend saunters over to the car.

Casually he gets in, and then a few moments later the car pulls away without the driver having ever looked in the rear view mirror first.

The resulting honking of hundreds of horns is the usual result. This cacophony of horn salutations by frustrated motorists is the expected result.

Adding to the confusion and chaos is the fact that Chinese motorists will honk their horns for literally, *'no reason at all.'* It just makes them feel important to honk the horns.

I have seen motorists honk their horns in echo to fireworks which happen to be going off in the area. China has a lot of fireworks!

Even though people are often injured or killed pulling such shenanigans it doesn't seem to affect the bulk of motorists as they seem completely incapable of learning from the mistakes of others or themselves. Thus, I call the Chinese *'The Un-Teachables'*.

EXAMPLE B. A bus driver decides he doesn't want to be behind another bus so he pulls out from behind him, never first looking, and occupies the next lane over.

At intersections one can often see four or five city buses standing five-abreast and blocking all traffic. As soon as the light turns green *"they're off and running."*

In the fury of screeching fan belts and clouds of dark diesel smoke the buses are off and running.

In their mad dash to *'get ahead'* they often miss the next bus stop so they have to *'back up'* several hundred feet in traffic to pick up their passengers.

There are few things more frightening and confusing than the back of a huge city bus headed straight for you at forty miles per hour and you're not even moving.

Bus drivers *'drag racing'* on the streets in the middle of the city is as common as horn honking. It happens all the time.

I won't go on, but suffice it to say that from 'U' turns in busy city traffic by buses to twenty-meter long lorries carrying gravel and occupying two lanes at a time, one can go mad watching and trying to drive around such nonsense.

CHAPTER 10

FALLOUT FROM THE 'ONE-CHILD POLICY'

RECENTLY RE-NAMED 'TWO-CHILD POLICY'.

TYRANNY BY ANY OTHER NAME.

DOOMED FROM BIRTH: As so many *'only children'* are being and have been born to Chinese society, it has left these children with an inability to learn through sibling example. This lack of sibling companionship has also denied their parents the ability to gain practical experience in child rearing.

The result has been that an overly coddled generation of children doted on by overly protective parents have already *'dumbed-down'* the Chinese people as a whole.

I see for myself, that a new phenomenon is occurring which threatens to further stupefy these already I.Q. impaired people. *That is the dissolution of extended family.* It's bad enough to be stupid from a large family of stupenagles, but to be an only child idiot must be unbearable.

DISSOLUTION OF THE FAMILY. Let me explain. For many generations, Mom and Dad lived with their children as they got older. This allowed Mom and Dad to help raise their grandchildren as they got older.

This also provided a social security net for Mom and Dad in their golden years. It was a terrific system and it worked! The typical Chinese family has changed over time, to something like this...

FAMILIES BEFORE CHINA'S DISASTROUS 'ONE-CHILD' POLICY. As China is largely an agrarian nation with nearly fifty percent of the population on the farm, I am mostly referring to those people who work and live in the cities.

I am not diminishing or belittling the farmers, but the fact is that China's college graduates, entrepreneurs, and future leaders are all coming from these *'city-raised'* families. This is by deliberate design of the Social Engineers of the Communist Party.

Note. Various legal and administrative restrictions keep the farmers from living or working in the cities. Beijing is loath to issue temporary resident visas to anyone from outside the city limits of any cities of size.

Mom, Dad, Sister, Brother, Little Brother, Grandma, Grandpa would made up a pretty typical family. Here we had four adults and three or four children. Well, the children benefitted from education via example from siblings, parents, and grandparents. China was strong socially.

Father worked full-time in employment outside the home and mother held down a part-time job of around 15 hours a week at most. Equally common was that mother would stay home in the full-time employment of raising a family. This was the Chinese Extended Family.

What this produced was well-balanced children, emotionally healthy parents, and the security provided by living with loving grandparents.

This was pretty much the universal Chinese model, a model still visible today in many Latin American countries and the Chinese Countryside.

THE FAMILY SINCE CHINA'S DISASTROUS SOCIAL POLICIES. Mom, Dad, Child, Grandma and Grandpa made up the typical family unit now. We find a shrinking family and a shrinking parental and grand-parental influence on the children. For that matter we see a shrinking child population and a growing population of senior citizens.

The kids are missing the benefits of sibling *'monkey see, monkey do'* education. These kids also have two working parents so their grandparents are pretty much raising them alone.

Grandpa and Grandma do as well as they can, but this system is no substitute for what they had before Deng Xiao Peng, *'The Butcher of Beijing'*, began to tinker with the most basic building block of society, the family.

This was before the greatest power grab in history, China's grab for the nation's very womb.

THE FAMILY AFTER PRESIDENT HU JIN TAO TOOK OFFICE AMID AN EXPANDING ECONOMY.

Mom, Dad, Child and possibly a single grandparent make up the family unit now. From extended to nuclear the family has changed greatly. This has proven disastrous to the strength of Chinese society as a whole, the family being the basic building block of any society.

The real problem here is that this nuclear family has only one child. The child is exposed to very limited peer relationships for any real childhood training.

These are those with any neighborhood kids who happen to be around, fewer and fewer as China's population ages and fewer and fewer children are born. The opportunity of growing up with peers is fast fading for a lot of Chinese children.

Both parents work, grandparents are mostly absent from the scene, and the child has no siblings. This has damaged basic education in so many ways because these kids are fighting an uphill struggle (*swimming up the waterfall*) having been deprived of all the advantages their parents and grandparents had when growing up.

The schools, especially primary schools, have been forced to adapt their curriculums to teach children basic social skills and manners. This instruction of social skills is necessitated as those children, those '*only children*', are picking up nothing from their parents who are too busy working or just too damned lazy to raise them.

OCS [*Only Child Syndrome*] has so damaged these kids emotionally and has contributed to their tremendous lack of interpersonal relationship skills. A lack of self-discipline has also reared its ugly head and rendered these children almost completely incapable of learning in school or on the job. They have become drones. *A society of drones cannot survive.*

Given these obvious handicaps, let's see what happens today, but let's add one more factor.

According to the Chinese Ministry of Public Security and Citizen Registration, the rate of divorce in China has skyrocketed from its single-digits of around seven percent in 2002 to well over thirty-four percent in 2014. This began to take place when Chinese courts recognized *'no fault'* divorce.

Now you've got *OCS* children living with a single parent, often missing the influence of a father altogether. In a nation where the ratio of boys to girls is two point three to one.

The percentage of single parents being women is ninety-three percent. This means there are too few men today to raise the men of tomorrow. This absence of a male role model already shows itself in many unpleasant ways in Chinese society.

A noticeable feminization of the Chinese male has taken place over the past twenty years and is most evident in those boys today under twenty years of age.

Homosexuality has exploded on the social scene much to Beijing's dislike, but directly a result of their social tampering.

AS YOU SEW, SO SHALL YOU REAP.

Long labeled a mental illness by Beijing, the condition of homosexuality [*arguably an acquired behavior*] has been on the increase and has forced Beijing to modify its stance on homosexuality slightly, and certainly will cause them to modify it more in the near future.

This and other factors make a recipe for disaster, a *'perfect storm'* of social unrest is the only certain result of such dramatic societal change.

LAMENTATIONS OF A NATION DESTROYED FROM WITHIN. In just thirty short years China has been shoehorned into the mold of the *'one-bedroom-family'* which is their term for a single-parent household.

The Chinese have come from large, extended families rich in tradition, culture, and discipline and have been crammed into families with insufficient leadership and love.

Gone is the wise and kindly influence of grandparents who can talk to a child when Mom and Dad are *'just a little busy right now'.* Gone is the experience and wisdom of age these grandparents once provided.

Missing from the lives of the young is the sage wisdom of age. Gone is the chance to seek the simple *'growing up'* wisdom of a sibling such as an older sister or brother.

Gone is the time Mother used to spend with each child or children in groups as she tended to the house or other children. Mom, it seemed, was always home.

Her day-to-day, moment-to-moment influence is no longer there for the children. Gone is that which once made China strong.

CHAPTER 11

CHINESE EDUCATION

MUCH ADO ABOUT NOTHING

NOTHING TO FEAR. In so many articles in so many newspapers and magazines around the world, we read of the '*Superior Education*' of the Chinese people. We are warned of the '*Coming Invasion of Chinese College Graduates*'.

I even read an article recently comparing Chinese universities with American Ivy League schools such as Princeton and Yale. What a bunch of rubbish!

We read how Chinese students continue to score higher in mathematics, science, and other key subjects than their western counterparts and how over eight hundred million Chinese are now studying English.

These facts and figures, on the surface, are impressive and intimidating and have probably scared many people in the west into fearing '*The Coming Colossus of China*'.

Let me assure you that such articles and stories are written by those who have never more than visited China and then probably on a guided tour.

Their knowledge of the Chinese people is clouded by their ignorance and over reliance on facts and figures from the Chinese government or worse, the American news media.

In fact, any such fear is horribly misplaced.

Any threat by their '*superior educations*' is the fabrication of fertile imaginations helped along with marvelous propaganda from Beijing and New York spin-doctors.

The fertilizer for this growing crop of lies is your ignorance. And you know what fertilizer is, right? Yep, shit! And the Chinese are full of it!

The truth is, the bulk of the Chinese people remain so intellectually and educationally handicapped as to be almost incapable of functioning even in their own world without constant supervision and direction. Their uncanny *inability* to learn, even by watching or doing, has led me to call them the '**The Unteachables.**'

A noted scholar, Doel Cam Nai, once said of China's teaching method, "*When you spend six years 'teaching to the test' even a monkey will score acceptably in a multiple-choice examination.*"

IMPOSSIBLE TO FAIL: This is the driving tenet of Chinese Education which has doomed it from its inception.

It's impossible to fail or even be '*held back*' in school in China. Parents and children are taught that '*all deserve to pass*' and that has become their mantra. Each parent and child has come to feel entitled to a passing grade whether it's earned or not.

Virtually everyone who starts the school year and doesn't die will graduate and be moved on to the next level. I mean *everyone*.

I can quote you case after case where a child has attended only '*opening class*' of the first semester and has graduated at the end of the year with an average grade of eighty-five percent or better! *The eighty-five percent figure is a default value assigned to students who fail to attend classes.*

Note. As a teacher I have to ask just one question of the many which burn holes in my brain, "Where did that figure of eighty-five percent come from?"

There are no standards in place to determine what is actually a '*pass*' and what is a '*fail*' so all children are simply '*moved along*' through the system. Says Doel Cam Nai, "*Under such a system as this, one could graduate a ham sandwich.*"

This silliness permeates the very essence of Chinese existence and has been with them for so long that nobody questions it. The fact is, this policy has been repeated with such unfailing regularity that even among top educational professionals in China it's accepted and regarded as '*the way things are done*'.

The '*impossible to fail*' system has been fully integrated and accepted without question as it continues to infect and destroy the very fabric of what is now laughingly called '*Chinese Education.*'

When I refer to *'the fabric'* I am speaking too loosely. The cloth of education, when there was one, has been reduced to tatters and can barely hold its own threadbare self together under the assault of the gale force winds of idiotic government policy.

LET'S START AT THE BEGINNING SHALL WE?

CHINESE NURSERY EDUCATION. From the beginning, as the Chinese put an even higher value on money than family, their children are almost immediately farmed out to nurseries around the country.

This is done typically at about the age of three. In these nurseries the children are baby-sat, but not really educated except in simple social etiquette and getting along with others. Not rocking the boat is a social *'must'* in Chinese Society and the children are well-drilled in the skills of social conformity.

As with most nurseries in China, and quite unlike many in the West, they are basically storage facilities for the yuppie-larvae of society.

These *'nurseries'* have very little do with actual child education or mental stimulation.

A typical middle or upper-class family will board their child from 6:30am until 6:30pm at least five or six days per week as they go off to their various jobs.

In return they are rewarded with emotionally retarded, socially crippled, robotically functioning, and frequently misbehaving children. So uniform is their maladjustment that they are almost uniformly *hedonistic, narcissistic Clones.*

The ingrained respect children usually have for their mother or father is often missing by age five.

By the time junior goes to first grade [*about age seven or eight*] he views his parents as his servants whose duty is to raise, feed, clothe, and pamper him. He has already developed a measurable level of contempt for his parents.

This is, in fact, the prevailing attitude and this attitude is actually reinforced through the government system of education. The result is a huge and burgeoning crop of spoiled brats, victims of *OCS* [*Only Child Syndrome*].

CHINESE PRIMARY SCHOOL EDUCATION. Okay, I concede. Here the Chinese do an excellent job and children receive a really first-rate basic education from caring and highly qualified teachers.

They are taught both social disciplines (*the behavioral rules their parents are too lazy and too busy to provide*) and the '*reading, writing, and arithmetic*' one would expect. There is a heavily propagandist slant pushing party and country as the final authority in life.

However, the Chinese indoctrination of the very young is much more intense than that of the west and painted with a much broader brush.

The children in Chinese Primary School do far more than 'Pledge Allegiance to the Flag." They practice close order drill and '*patriotic*' song and dance regularly.

Recently the new administration of China's President Xi has made the teachings of The Party, Karl Marx, Mao, and Confucius mandatory at all levels of public education.

Another major difference here is that in China, *'different'* or *'unique'* in a child is not acceptable. This *'anomaly'* is dealt with swiftly and harshly.

Corporal punishment in the Primary School System is used widely and with some degree of abandon. This is the only truly structured and disciplined education the Chinese child will ever receive.

• **DON'T ASK QUESTIONS.** Here it's driven into their tiny growing minds, from the very first day of school, that asking questions is tantamount to challenging the teacher.

It's often considered an insult to a teacher to ask her or him a question and the child is left to simply *'work this out for himself'* which often means the child comes to erroneous conclusions or simply discards the question and moves on to the next problem.

In essence, it never happens. The child quickly learns that memorization is preferable to actually thinking. All learning is by wrote. This system is one of memorization rather than actual learning.

• **NEVER QUESTION AUTHORITY.** The teacher is always right ... *always*. Children are taught to take as *'gospel'* all that comes from the textbooks and the teachers who teach from them. When they are told to do something, anything at all, it's to be done immediately and without question or wondering why.

• **INDEPENDENT THOUGHT IS DANGEROUS.** *"Ideas are dangerous things."* is a motto, a mantra taught them every day. When a child has an inkling of an idea which might improve or streamline a process of any kind it's immediately stifled.

Independent thought is discouraged in every possible way. It's said, *"This is how we have always done it. Who are you to question the ways of thousands of years of civilization?"*

As a result, the primary schools in China do turn out well-versed little drones who can do their math, understand general science, and have a fair verbal command over much of the simplified language which most Chinese speak, read and write.

At the close of a primary school education, each student takes a national examination which determines the middle school he or she will be allowed to attend.

Chinese schools don't bear names, but rather numbers. It's every parent's dream to have their child admitted to #1 Middle School of their town.

When the resulting test scores are not quite right, Mom's and Dad's wallets open up and many of these children still attend the #1 Middle School. However, while Primary Education is free in China, Middle School Education is not! There are no *'financial aid'* programs for the poor. **Pay up or push off!**

It's interesting that the education these children received for free in their first six years of school is significantly superior to what they are about to pay *'top dollar'* for in middle and high school.

It's not uncommon at all for parents to buy or rent a home near their child's primary school to ensure an efficient and short trip to and from school by their children during these *'critical'* first six years of education.

I have even seen mothers take local jobs, menial in nature, in order to stay closer to the school and monitor the situation at hand. *Also under this all is that fact that Chinese parents simply don't trust their children.* Keeping their children busy under the front of '*extra study classes*' is just that, a front.

Teachers also tend to live close to their schools and as children always take '*extra classes*' daily in teachers' homes it makes even more sense to live as near to school [*and the teachers' homes*] as possible.

By '*education*' I mean, memorization for the Middle School Entrance Examination which is the exam that determines what Middle School the child will attend. The entire final year of Primary School is spent memorizing answers for the upcoming exam.

Sample exams are given monthly, and all children are drilled to score highly on the test. They are not learning a thing, they are simply memorizing the questions and the answers.

Primary School children attend school from Monday through Friday, 7:30am until 3:30pm. Weekend school is around holidays when '*makeup classes*' are required, it happens frequently. These '*makeup classes*' are meant to replace days missed from the school year caused by any holidays *There really are no 'days off' in China's school system.*

An interesting note is that the very small (*I do mean small, as they are almost unnoticeable in the population*) population of minorities gets a lot smaller when a child enters middle school, a lot smaller!

Most primary schools will not admit any darker-skinned minorities. Those such as Uighur children are routinely refused admission.

The Uighur are a brown-skinned Arabic race. While some semi-rural school will occasionally allow the Uighur to attend at the Primary level, that's as far as it goes.

Darker-skinned minorities are openly discouraged from attending alongside the *whiter, and hence superior, children.* These being the children of the Han tribe.

MIDDLE SCHOOL. This is where failure of *'the system'* begins to show itself in wholesale fashion. It's here, in grades seven through nine that the school system breaks down into the irreparable mess it has become today. Any possibility of a child having independent thought or using his imagination are finally laid to rest.

'Stepping outside the box' in any way is finally locked down and destroyed. It's here that any potential for originality or individuality is finally crushed.

TOO CROWDED. Even in a *'Number One'* highest rated middle school, class sizes will range from fifty to eighty students on a regular basis.

Class length is forty minutes, which means that the teacher really has no time to *'teach'*, but rather only time to *'review'* previous work and possibly answer one or two basic questions related directly to the text at hand.

The teacher is inundated with daily lecture duties and the need to grade hundreds of test papers weekly. It's not uncommon for an

English teacher to sit up nights in her home until midnight each night grading papers.

Students take fairly major tests bi-weekly and even larger ones monthly. Checking homework takes so much of a teacher's time that he or she has no time to actually teach.

TEACHERS DON'T TEACH. Teachers are also paid on the low-end of the professional pay scale. A seasoned veteran of fifteen years will receive around six hundred dollars [*U.S. Currency equivalent*] per month which will support her and her child, but there isn't much left to spare. She will usually supplement her income handsomely by tutoring children in her home.

Middle School children typically attend school from Monday through Saturday on weekdays from 7:30 till 5:30pm. Sundays are spent in school from 9am till 5pm.

At this point in his life, the typical student will also attend an average of twelve hours class time in teachers' homes for tutorial private instruction of various subjects.

This tutoring is supposedly to help *'give them an edge'* in the extremely competitive High School Entrance Exams to be held every June.

Let's remember that *'giving them an edge'* is only one of the two main reasons a child spends his every off-school hour in a teacher's home.

It's largely because the parents don't trust their children and this is a way of providing them with *'baby-sitting'* while the parents save face.

After all, it wouldn't do to tell your neighbors that your fourteen year old son is at a babysitter's house. No, he is *'in class'*. Sounds better, don't you think?

This also provides a way for teachers to make a good income teaching in their homes. An English teacher, for example, can make five times her official salary by tutoring in the home.

Many teachers *'require'* this extracurricular study with the threat of not getting into a decent high school.

The daily routine for a teacher is to have students copy what has been written on the blackboard in detailed notes. Then the teacher will randomly ask a few students to clarify a piece of the work on the board.

By this time, the music is playing (*rather than using a bell, most schools play snippets of baroque music to announce beginning and end of class periods*) and the teacher has time enough only to assign homework, that is all.

Class is over!

The next time class is in session, the teacher collects the homework, asks a few basic questions to clarify a few areas of the homework which had been assigned, and then the students again copy what has been written on the blackboard.

The cycle goes on with exams being the only interruptions.

UNDERPAID AND UNDER-QUALIFIED. Teachers often teach with less than a Bachelor's Degree (*a certification from* *a two-year teacher's college is normal)* and almost never teach in the field of their major.

TEACHERS OFTEN HAVE TO BUY THEIR JOBS. At the cost of a year's wages, a teacher may often '*buy the job*' from the headmaster or headmistress who simply pockets the cash and sacks someone on staff to make room for the new teacher.

The '*sacked-one*' is usually one who has not previously purchased their job or someone who has, but it has been fairly recent [*only a few years*] and the headmaster is willing to weather the storm when he or she fires that teacher to '*make room*'for the new one ... for the new money.

GOOD OLD-FASHIONED BRIBES. Known as an '*honour offerings*' most teachers will readily take bribes of sometimes thousands of U.S. Dollars in exchange for giving students higher grades.

Teachers will alter test scores of the paying students once an '*honor offering*' has been received. The resulting higher scores ensure a child's progress in class and keeps parents happy.

Rather than being discouraged from this practice, teachers often attend seminars on how to better organize their graft. Corruption is so deeply ingrained in Chinese society that this isn't questioned by anyone. After all, this is how they have done it for thousands of years.

AN ALARMING LACK OF FACILITIES. In Chinese Middle Schools, the lack of facilities is alarming, at best, with most schools having no lunch rooms and insufficient toilet stalls indoors or immediately outside. The unsanitary nature of a Chinese public lavatory is frightening, especially in the schools. Let the wind shift during class on a hot day and classes close for a while.

These bathrooms never have hot running water or toilet paper. It's **BYOP** (*Bring your own paper*) across the board nationwide.

These toilets in use are the Arabian-style squat toilets which are really nothing more than a porcelain-lined hole in the floor. In most schools there are no doors on the stalls. In about half the schools there are no walls for stalls at all.

There are no stalls, period. The urinal in a boys' room will be a long trench along the wall with running water pouring down the back wall into the trough.

NOBODY WASHES THEIR HANDS.

INSUFFICIENT HEALTHCARE AND MEDICAL FACILITIES. In a school of three thousand students or more there is nobody with any medical training at all, not even Basic First Aid.

To find a first aid kit anywhere in the school would be as common as stumbling across a three pound gold nugget in your underwear.

I've found a few nuggets in my underwear, but I assure you they've never been made of gold!

If a child arrives at school pale, shaking, perspiring, and coughing he is still required to attend class as the others do. In any western school, children are sent home for a fraction of these symptoms, but not in China.

The rule of thumb here is, *"If you can walk, you can learn."* and this has led to so many mass infectious disease outbreaks and epidemics in China that it would take another book just to cover them.

Suffice it to say that it's not uncommon for schools to close for days as an influenza epidemic or other such thing as measles, chicken pox, etc. ravages the school population and the local community.

HERE'S THE REAL CLINCHER. Once the epidemic has passed, the students will work extra weekends and holidays to make up for the days they missed from school! *Schools receive their annual funding based on attendance and days taught,* so the incentive is to pack those classrooms whether the kids are dead and dying or not.

The fault for this lies equally between administrators, teachers, and parents. The parents are using the school as a *'baby-sitter'* and don't want to take their *'precious time'* looking after a sick child. After all, Chinese employers don't pay *'sick leave'.*

Administrators are rewarded based on school attendance and don't want to lose any of their year-end bonus money either.

The teachers simply follow in lock-step with their leaders because that's the way things are done.

Besides, a teacher who doesn't follow along is in danger of *'getting the sack'.* Whatever reason a teacher may have been fired [*sacked*] for, getting another job is next to impossible.

SCIENCE CLASSES. Imagine attending a Chemistry class and not having a sink, Bunsen burner, or any test tubes. *Welcome to China!* This is how it's.

Chemistry class consists of information written on the blackboard and the students taking copious notes so they can memorize the information and spit it back onto a test paper later on.

Most kids enter university Chemistry classes having never even seen a test tube outside the venue of a grade 'B' horror film.

MUSIC INSTRUCTION. No musical instruments are available for general use. The few instruments here are usually the personal property of individual *'special'* students who are *'connected'*.

There is a 'music room' but its use is reserved for members of the school orchestra and select teachers.

Again, a case of *'memorize and regurgitate'* because *'hands on'* just doesn't happen in the Chinese education system.

TEACHING TO THE TEST. T2T. This is how done. All subjects are taught in order to supply the exact answers. The *'teaching'* is a preparation for students to memorize the precise information required to pass all exams.

As expected, most students forget everything they had *memorized* once they have completed the test. It's normal human nature to discard any information the brain no longer sees a need for.

The actual tests and exams are generally very poorly written and completely inadequate to the task of evaluating a student's understanding or knowledge in any particular subject area. As a result, the middle schools of China continue to turn out a mediocre and undereducated crop of students year after year.

Through inadequate curriculum, unqualified teachers, inadequate facilities, overcrowded schools, and a complete lack of imagination or creative thought, the students leaving middle school for high school are ill-prepared at best, and doomed to failure at worst.

At the close of a middle school education, each student takes a national examination also called the Zhong Kao (*pronounced "Johng Cow"*) that determines which high school he or she will be allowed to attend.

The High Schools don't bear names, but rather numbers, as with their middle school counterparts. It's every parent's dream to have their child admitted to #1 High School.

Sound familiar? Also, *'passing'* Middle School isn't the issue. This is China. *Nobody ever fails. Nobody can fail. Nobody will ever fail.*

REMEMBER. *"You could graduate a ham sandwich at any grade in Chinese Public Schools. Add a little mustard and cheese and you've got a valedictorian!"*

When the test scores are *'not quite right'*, parents' wallets once again open up and many low-scoring kids will still attend the #1 High School. Any student must be from a family of means in order to attend High School as it can be quite expensive.

It's interesting to note a complete lack of minorities in middle or high school. These schools are the domain of the ruling Chinese, and minorities are simply not tolerated. I have toured and taught in dozens of #1 High Schools across China and can't remember ever seeing even one minority student or teacher.

HIGH SCHOOLS. These are, at best, a tragedy. The culmination of the previous three years of learning by wrote and memorization for the sake of memorization now come to a head. Here, virtually all three years of schooling are spent in preparation for the Gao Kao (*Pronounced "Gow Cow"*) exam.

The Gao Kao is the Universal College Entrance Examination and determines a student's university or college choice as well as their major. Cheating on this exam is widespread.

This cheating, which has gone on throughout primary and middle school becomes far more visible and shows a greater prevalence in high school. *"Cheating"* means *"getting ahead"* in Chinese society and is never frowned upon.

So tolerated is this cheating that even when a student is caught red-handed, there is no reprisal and often not even a mention from teacher to student.

Their cheating is not always a surreptitious act, and is often so obvious as to almost challenge a teacher to say something. The quickest way to the unemployment line for a teacher is to nab a cheater, especially if the cheater's parents are *'connected'* with friends in the right places.

The Gao Kao, according to many senior education officials and teachers with whom I have consulted, is subject to such widespread cheating by nearly eighty percent of students taking this *'all important'* exam.

In one way or another, they all do. Cheating is generally accomplished by purchasing the answers online or from a favorite teacher. There are also *'cram'* classes in teachers' homes where the questions and answers are drilled and driven into the students.

In recent years the cram classes have grown in popularity as cheating has become more difficult and infinitely more expensive. A set of exam answers can run over six-thousand United States Dollars and may be only about eighty percent correct.

Even the exam itself is published by a private firm with close ties to national government where '*the fix is in*' so as to retain their monopoly on testing for college entrance. This same firm also which published books on how to '*cram for the exam*'.

These books often contain the very questions and answers which will be in the upcoming Gao Kao Exam. The taking of the Gao Kao is a nationally celebrated annual event with police closing off entire avenues as schools go into lockdown.

Tens of thousands of parents camp outside the schools in a festival atmosphere awaiting the start and finish of this all-important exam. Entire industries orbit the Gao Kao.

As the children are indoors, often with no air-conditioning, on a hot June day taking their exams, parents patiently wait.

One can see parents sitting on folding chairs under umbrellas sipping juices and tea, snacking on cakes, buying souvenirs from local vendors, and having a jolly good time of it.

As relatives swap lies about their yuppie larvae, the students inside are knuckling down for the most important exam of their lives. Parents spend the day chatting up their friends and neighbors on the wonderful qualities of their children or grandchildren, whoever is taking this most coveted of test on this special day.

Throughout the year parents have paid teachers enormous sums to tutor their children after school on answer preparation for this exam. Often, equally enormous sums have gone into paying bribes to the '*right people*' to ensure a good outcome of the exam.

YOUR TICKET TO THE GOOD LIFE … A COLLEGE EDUCATION. Chinese universities pay huge sums to local school districts nationwide in order to ensure that *'the need of a university education'* is always stressed. This keeps the universities in fresh supplies of new students every September.

This continual and repetitive process of indoctrination is only a small part of their ongoing media campaign. *"If you tell a lie enough, it becomes truth."*

They use multimedia and even organized *'word of mouth'* campaigns for spreading misinformation and imaginary factoids. This is so as to convince parents everywhere that their children will end up on the streets selling matches or recycling beer cans if they don't get into a good university.

CHINESE UNIVERSITIES. These are a complete and utter sham. A disaster already made and being nurtured by all of Chinese society, the universities shoehorn themselves into the very lives of gullible Chinese parents.

It's not unfair to say that a university education in China is not even up to the level of a high school education as it was in the United States or United Kingdom back in the mid 1970s.

Worse yet, it's commonly believed that a college education has become *'critical to the future of China'*. Virtually everything said by the university industry is accepted without question. Nobody dares challenge the education industry, as they are after all … the educated ones. *"If you tell a lie often enough, it becomes fact."*

Universities in China are, like their high school counterparts, impossible to fail. If you get in, pay your fees, and attend even a few of your classes, a Bachelor Degree is assured. I mean **assured.**

The fact is that attendance is not mandatory. Payment of fees and payment of an *'honorarium'* to the school at the end of four years grants you a diploma.

As in all the Chinese education system, nobody ever fails. *Where's that ham sandwich?*

Inadequate curriculum, disorganized administration, a *'no-fail'* policy, overcrowding, and widespread corruption cause Chinese Universities to be no more than diploma mills with dormitories and desks.

These mills crank out many tens of millions of Bachelor Degrees every year and an unemployment rate of over eighty percent is the reward a graduate receives for his *'effort'*.

I taught at China's premier mainland university for more than one year, and was shocked at the lax, laisser-faire atmosphere among the students and staff. Being a *'no-fail'* establishment, there is no real incentive for students to work hard or for staff to ply the challenging art of education.

The few times I actually gave students a failing grade, I was chastised by administration and the student's grades were altered accordingly. It was then that I began writing this book.

It was common for these students (*in an honors class*) to pay others to write their papers and even take their exams for them. There are flourishing firms surrounding the campuses of most major universities which openly offer these services.

One time, when presented with a number of papers to grade, I noticed that about a third of them were written by the same hand and, were in fact, the same papers.

The students had all paid the same firm to '*write*' their papers and the firm had chosen only a few papers to mass copy for the dozens of students who had solicited their services.

ITS NOT JUST THE STUDENTS WHO DON'T BELONG IN COLLEGE. I worked alongside the Dean of the Linguistics Department whose qualification was a B.A. majoring in Computer Science. His Chinese wasn't very good, his English was far worse, and he spoke no other language. He was only in his early thirties. Gee, I suppose he '*got lucky*'.

This is indicative of the type of placements made on the staff of Chinese universities at large.

In need of a complete overhaul that will never happen, the University System in China is a burgeoning industry and continues to crank out diplomas en masse. They rake in huge sums artfully spreading their propaganda which ensures a steady stream of new students and freshman money.

If you're one of those worry-mongers who are afraid that the U.K. or U.S. are falling behind the Chinese academically, don't be alarmed. I assure you that there is nothing to worry about! Yes, the U.K. and U.S. do have horrible education systems. Education in the west has slipped to all-time lows.

The public education systems of the U.K. and U.S. have their own wide range of problems, this is a fact. But rest assured that our problems are miniscule when compared to the jungle of the Chinese system.

While all attempts to repair public education in the west have thus far failed, remember that China's situation and status are still far, far worse. This is because China doesn't recognize there is a problem.

The Chinese are in complete denial! At least in the West we admit *[at least to ourselves]* that our education system is in trouble. Sleep soundly tonight, comforted in the knowledge that there will not be a hoard of highly educated, imaginative, clever and motivated Chinese flooding the land and taking our jobs. Sleep well. You are safe. The sky is not falling.

'MAINSTREAMING'. Now, I am not nor have I ever been an advocate of the policy of *'mainstreaming'* which is the disturbing practice of inserting handicapped children into *'mainstream'* schools and classes, seemingly regardless of the level of handicap or challenge the student faces.

This practice has proven to be an abject failure by any definition. It has also been proven disastrously detrimental to the performance of the student body and their respective schools at large. One look at such efforts in America and Canada serves as a testament to the lunacy of these programs.

Most teachers find that mainstreaming greatly diminishes their own teaching effectiveness.

China is certainly not guilty of anything even resembling *'mainstreaming'*.

In China, if your eyesight is not correctable to a functional level you are shuffled off to a *special* school. The same is automatic for any physical deformity which might offend the delicate sensibilities of other students or their parents.

I have had the misfortune of touring many of the *'special needs' schools* built to accommodate these children and they can best be described as *'dungeons with blackboards ... staffed by teachers with even blacker hearts.'*

I just don't have room in this book to elucidate on these remedial hell-holes.

It seems they also provide a very cheap [*even by Chinese standards*] source of labor for many overseas firms such as medical equipment companies requiring simple assembly or sporting goods manufacturers requiring simple assembly-line stitching and gluing.

I toured a *'school for the blind'* where I saw dozens of children locked in rooms where they sewed footballs and running shoes with famous name labels on them.

Somehow I doubt this was part of an *'on the job training program'*.

Far more can be said of the dreadful conditions of these places where the *'useless'* of society are hidden away during their formative years only to be transferred to an adult facility at age sixteen.

ONE LESS MOUTH TO FEED. Rarely, and I mean rarely, one makes it through the system as a result of the loving and dedicated efforts of parents who are accomplished at home schooling.

HOME SCHOOLING THE INFIRM. Thankfully, there are parents who find these murderous practices unacceptable and decide to keep and raise their children. There is something to be said for this.

A parent's love for her child only grows as time passes, regardless of infirmity or deformity. A lucky few handicapped will enjoy a mother's touch at home for however long they shall live.

A simple survey shows that, among my own many university students and acquaintances, none has ever had a relationship with a severely handicapped person. I have asked, believe me, and very few [*perhaps one in a thousand*] can even recall seeing a handicapped person in their neighborhood or school.

I was blessed to be part of a situation where the parents of about a dozen or so severely handicapped children had joined forces to home-school their children. It was working very well and I eagerly volunteered my services as an English teacher.

Some of the best moments of my life in the decades I have spent in China were in that little one-room schoolhouse.

I found myself surrounded by warm and caring, intelligent adults and angelic children pursuing a dream.

Well, I will never fully understand why, but about a year was as long as it lasted before city authority came through and *'disbanded'* the school.

The school was broken up, literally, by thugs with clubs who waded through the classroom one Monday morning knocking over desks, breaking chairs and threatening handicapped children and their parents.

We were accused of participating in an unauthorized gathering and establishment of an unauthorized organization dispensing uncensored information. In China it's a felony to teach from *'unapproved'* texts. It falls under the *'Child Abuse'* laws.

IT HAPPENS EVERY DAY. The *'approved'* special schools and institutions live in a constant state of epidemic where *'accidental deaths'* and *'suicides'* proliferate.

Among students this *epidemic of death* has yet to be addressed by government. I suppose to Beijing this means there is *'One less mouth to feed.'*

This is the government that recently boasted of *'having prevented four-hundred million births'* since the inception of its infamous *'One-Child'* Policy.

The Communist government actually brags about forced abortions [*I have seen this happen even in the 8th month of gestation!*] and mandatory sterilization of *'certain people'*.

Can you think of a more terrifying control of the people than to reach into the very womb of society to decide who will be born and who will not? Whoa!

What is thought of as a horrible and unconscionable evil by we people of the west is considered 'business as usual' by the Han Chinese by and large. <u>We are not the same</u>!

In China, the *'accidental death'* and *'suicide'* rates in these special school run over one thousand percent the rate of children in *'normal'* schools.

From the airports to the schools, from restaurants to shopping malls, from trains to taxis one sees and hears of only two token efforts on the part of the Chinese government which are put to the public as *'significant efforts to aid the handicapped'*.

CHAPTER 12
RELIGION & ETHICS IN CHINA
"LIFE WITHOUT A MORAL COMPASS"

MAO STARTED IT ALL. I can only guess why these people seem completely without morals or any standards of '*right*' and '*wrong*'. Any strong ethos can be traced to religion, belief in God, etc. In China, this is an element missing from society.

Ever since the reign of the murderous and terrible Chairman Mao who ruled and ruined the land and the minds of the people, religion has died.

At the end of a gun barrel, a bayonet, or a hangman's noose, Mao systematically purged organized religion from the land. Even the invasion of Tibet was designed to serve the eventual goal of Mao which was to *"Eliminate all religion at all costs."*

EMPEROR MAO'S SUCCESS. Through the period known in China as, *"The Great Leap Forward"*, monasteries and churches were torn down, monks and nuns raped, tortured, brutalized and murdered, and the people at large threatened with worse if they harbored thoughts of or openly worshipped a God.

The succeeding period of time known in China as, *"The Cultural Revolution"* successfully cemented the goals of the now aging and increasingly senile Chairman Mao. A tyrant cum madman now finishing his work even as he was dying.

While Mao's true cause of death is still unclear, it's believed by many [*and for good reason*] that he was killed by the Party as he had seized too much power. Many at that time felt that Mao Ze Dong's ego was slowly, but surely driving China into the abyss.

The *'slow poisoning'* theory is upheld by two of his former physicians as well as his personal manservant. The reign of China's last emperor was over.

REMAINING OPINIONS OF CHAIRMAN MAO. Those in China aged fifty-five years and over well remember the Cultural Revolution. Those over seventy well remember the atrocities and acts of murderous intent that so marked this dark period of China's history, the remnants of which continue to be seen today.

A simple *'sit-down'* with any group of older retirees will reveal horror stories and tales that would turn your hair whiter than mine. It was a time of terror.

IN PLAIN SIGHT. In China today we see thousands of churches dotting the land. Catholic, Baptist, Buddhist, Muslim, and *One-Size-Fits-All* churches are to be seen everywhere sporting the cross on a steeple or a statue of Buddha in the courtyard. To the tourist or the totally ignorant, this is a great sign of progress in the dictatorship of China. Unfortunately, *this is not a good sign.*

These churches are the tools of the Party and well designed to show the world that *"China 'encourages' religion and religious behavior and belief among its people."*

All churches in China, with the exception of those secret and underground groups, the clandestine worshippers, are nothing more than empty buildings constructed, owned, and operated by the People's Communist Party of Beijing, the true power in China.

From the centers of religious authority around the world, all these churches are roundly denounced and decried as *'fake'*, like so many things that China does, not real, just poor copies of the real thing.

These *'churches'* are minimally staffed and go to great lengths to appear genuine in their trappings, furniture arrangements, and heavily edited copies of The Holy Bible and The Quran laying on seats, rugs, and pews.

THE RESULT. With no religion or organized system for the teaching of religious principles, the Chinese have developed a culture without order and without a sense of right and wrong. It's a culture of chaos.

THE MOST COMMON RULES OF SOCIETY SEEM TO BE CLEAR, ALTHOUGH DEFINITELY WARPED.

ONE IDEA. Telling a lie to a family member is not cool, and is in fact frowned upon unless there is *some obvious and enviable benefit* to be had, then okay. If, by lying to a family member, it puts you very much ahead in position, power, or wealth, then you are justified.

ANOTHER IDEA. Telling a lie to one who is not Han is yet another thing. It's an almost comical series of events to watch the Han as they try to cheat minorities in any way they can.

It's comical because the minorities, especially the Uighur, are generally smarter, quicker, and far more savvy than their Han counterparts. Many Uighur people take delight in watching a Han man or woman making fools of themselves as they try to weave a lie or to cheat one of the Uighur people.

The gene pool of the Uighur is far deeper than that of the Han, the culture is richer and much less adulterated. The Uighur, by and large, have a strong moral compass born of their roots in Islam and to a lesser degree in Christianity.

The physical size, violent temperament, and willingness to readily die for Allah made the Uighur people a *'hands-off'* thing for the Communist Government of China. The Uighur live in their own little world, a world within the Han world, yet separate and far from it.

The Uighur have their own rules of society, conduct business almost exclusively among themselves, and are quite wary of dealing with the Han in any way.

The Uighur are a growing power in small business in China. They own and operate small supermarkets, delicatessens, restaurants, and other small businesses.

If a Uighur attends university, which is quite rare, it's out of province and paid for entirely by the family. This young man will return from college to help in the family business.

More and more of their children who seek a college education [*not many see the need*] attend universities overseas.

Always, they attend church and adhere to the religious principles of their own faith. The Uighur are predominantly Muslim, but there are also a fair number of Uighur Christians.

The way these minorities of China are treated today is even worse than how the United States treats its native people.

Officially licensed and sanctioned churches in China preach sermons, all carefully edited and censored (*often written*) by party officials. To vary from the script will cost a *'minister'* his job, his freedom, perhaps his life.

Hence, morality and religion in China aren't quite dead, but they are in critical condition. Islam in China largely escapes this travesty of condition.

GOD IS NOT DEAD, NOT EVEN IN CHINA. Well, here we go into the really gritty stuff. Two churches vex China greatly as they operate either secretly or in direct defiance of the powers-that-be.

ISLAM. The church operates out of mosques which are closely monitored, often with 24-hour surveillance in place. All persons entering and leaving are photographed and records kept at the Public Security Bureau.

This is because, some years ago, Beijing lost a great deal of control of the Islamic population. The people were being taught by visiting teachers from Turkey, Pakistan, and Mongolia.

These *'visiting teachers'* still slip in to this day and leak teachings from unedited copies of the Quran, their holy book of scripture.

Islam in China is a quiet and peaceful variant of the faith, even more so than is Islam in Turkey, and that suits Beijing just fine as they well know the resolve of militant Islam. Beijing considers themselves lucky that they are dealing with a more *'controllable'* variant of Islam on their turf.

FALUN DAFA ~ FALUN GONG: This is a new-age / Hinduesque religion born in China during the 1970's in the wake of Chairman Mao's death. It grew like wildfire, at one time claiming over 500 million members.

Its teachings were benign and all related toward the spreading of peace and love. This faith was, surprisingly, embraced by the Communist Party.

The leader of this church, Mr. Li, was frequently awarded and showered with accolades by the Chinese government at all levels. Beijing even went so far as to issue special printings of currency sporting the sunrise symbol of the Falun Gong.

Seeing that this church had pacified many pockets of resistance to government and had indeed pacified the people at large, the party viewed it as a valuable tool. The Falun Gong were viewed as being invaluable in population management. Control has always been the goal of the Communist Party.

However, sitting in the wings and awaiting his turn at bat, a man named Deng Xiao Peng was poised and ready to strike at the heart of the Falun Gong church.

Deng waited for his chance to get at the church which he despised, loathed, and hated to an unbelievable degree.

During his time before election to Chairman of the Communist Party, he kept many of these thoughts to himself but, as Chief of the Army, he was not without influence.

Across the land, hundreds of millions of people practiced the prayers and faith of Falun Gong ~ Falun Dafa. China was finding herself. A sense of morality even began to poke its head above the ground where it had long hibernated under the tyranny of the Communist boot.

DENG MAKES HIS MOVE. Shortly after becoming president and party chairman, Deng made his move. He began to subtly dig at the church of Falun Gong in his speeches and public addresses, testing the waters of the people to see just how far he could go.

Being a mostly apathetic people by nature and rearing, the Chinese people did not react in a negative way, or in any way for that matter. It seemed for a while that Deng's words fell on deaf ears.

Under Deng's direction the government controlled - owned - news media began a quiet series of reports looking into *'the dark side of Falun Gong'.*

The news reports and other brilliantly written propaganda pieces began to work, and the tide of public opinion slowly turned from open approval to suspicious, fear and an apprehensive intolerance toward the Falun Gong sect.

THE TIME WAS RIGHT. Deng arranged for CCTV News (*China's only source of television*) to show Falun Gong members burning themselves alive in Beijing in public protest. A closer inspection of the video would have shown these self-immolations as originating in the nation of Nepal.

Deng had the images he needed to scare the pants off the people.

Deng probably learned his media savvy from the United States where Hollywood brainwashes the world daily. The media reported the alleged deaths of children whom church practitioners had allegedly denied medication in favor of religious methodologies such as prayer, etc.

As in the U.K. and U.S.A. people are suckers for whatever they see or hear in major media and a fear began to engulf the people of China.

If you remember the fiasco at Waco, Texas where government troops murdered men, women, and children at the Branch Davidian Compound you can see a reflection of what worked for Deng Xiao Peng in China.

In some ways, people are all the same. We are gullible, too trusting, and we have an almost mindless worship of major media.

THE DENG PURGES BEGAN. These came in a tidal wave of crushing force from the pen of Chairman Deng. Swiftly and without mercy, soldiers of the People's Liberation Army moved throughout the land in a door-to-door sweep.

Arrests, beatings, killings, were common during this time. Soldiers kicked down doors and dragged entire families out into the streets. These were, after all, the Falun Dafa. They were the enemies of the state and therefore the enemies of the people.

In a matter of only weeks, it was over. Millions of Chinese were arrested, executed, tortured, beaten, imprisoned, sentenced to re-education, or driven to escape China for refuge in other lands.

The great purge did away with any remaining good will the public might have had toward the Falun Gong. The once-awarded and revered church was now a vile and detested thing, a pariah. Falun Gong remain a hiss and a by-word in China.

As in Waco, Texas and other such incidents where the government wanted public support before committing atrocities, this formula worked well. ***It still does ...***

STEP ONE. *Sew rumors of the detestability of a group or organization. Attribute practices or beliefs to these people that the general populace would consider repugnant.*

STEP TWO. *Spread rumors of heinous acts this group commits against their own and others. Include women, children, and the elderly as 'victims' in your 'news reporting'.*

STEP THREE. *Report on major media the crimes this group is supposedly committing. Make up some really repulsive crimes. Those involving sex, children, and drugs are all good for this purpose. Make true Media Circus.*

In other words, use the media to vilify, dehumanize, and then turn the *'enemy'* into a *'threat to public peace, safety and decency.'*

Doel Cam Nai once said, *"People are generally stupid and will believe anything the major media tells them."* It has always worked for governments to secure public support before they eliminate a foe.

"Demonize, Isolate, Attack." That's the mantra. From Nero of Rome and his persecution of the Christians to Chairman Deng's slaughter of the innocents, this is a *'sure-fire'* formula.

WHY DID DENG GO AFTER THE FALUN GONG? First, remember that this is the same guy who in 1989 ordered the murder of thousands of unarmed and peaceful protesters (*many of them college kids*) in Tiananmen Square in Beijing.

This was a man jealous of the love of the people who could never be allowed follow anyone else. For any groups such as this *'church'* to share any of Deng's own *'divine'* glory with another God was unbearable. Yes, Chairman Deng fancied himself a God.

"The Party is God." He had said again and again. His *'religion'* was that which could be delivered at the point of a bayonet or the barrel of a gun.

Today hundreds of millions of Falun Gong meet secretly in homes, tents, abandoned buildings and in caves, waiting for the one day when they may see freedom of religion.   going to be a long wait!

Again, in fear of increased oppression, the people abandoned the thin veneer of morality which the Falun Dafa ~ Falun Gong had begun to paint on the hearts of the people.

This served as proof and solid confirmation to the Chinese people that their old ways of lying, cheating, and deceit were indeed the only truths one could safely embrace.

To this day, the Falun Gong are regarded by Mainlanders as liars, thieves, and even murderers. In fact they are simply a neo-new age quasi hinduesque group of folks with some rather exotic views on life and the spirit.

THERE YOU HAVE IT. With Islam intimidating Beijing into an uneasy standoff, and Falun Dafa ~ Falun Gong in hiding, there are no *real* churches of any kind.

The people of China have no guideposts or other sources of truth from which a moral compass can be crafted or calibrated. China is a land without morality. They exist only in the light of subjective opportunism and the lies of the Communist Party of China.

CHAPTER 13

LEGACY OF A FAILED POLICY DECISION

The disintegration of society and the demise of the family unit really began in China in 1979 when Deng Xiao Peng helped usher in the draconian measures of a national *One-Child* policy.

This was a policy which included imprisonment, forced abortion, re-education, even execution of violators who dared have an 'unauthorized child'.

The atrocities committed by China to enforce this edict are numerous and varied, and always frightening. They continue to this day and even Deng Xiao Peng's *'tour de force'* at Tiananmen pales in comparison to the onerous 'One-Child' Policy.

Rather than to control excess population, the true reason for this policy was one of control of the people, an all-present stranglehold on the most basic unit of society, the family.

After all, what control is more basic than control of the womb of every woman in China!

When a government is so empowered as to decide who will and who will not be born, then they have achieved *'absolute'* power.

They have licensed and begun to govern creation itself! With a government as hungry for total control as is Beijing, this policy was bound to become a reality sooner or later.

SUMMARY OF SIN. Today, after various revisions made to the disastrous 'One-Child' policy, about forty-nine percent of Chinese are still covered under the conditions imposed by the *One-Child policy.

Note. Recently the Central Government of China announced cessation of their One-Child Policy, making it now a 'Two-Child Policy'. However, they made this announcement prematurely and have since announced that the change of policy will go up for final review sometime the next year.

Government has urged all local governments and jurisdictions to "... continue to police and enforce existing policies in the matter of child-birth with utmost diligence and severity."

This policy is also riddled with *'back doors and loopholes'* allow-ing the wealthy (*China's Royalty*) to circumvent the policy through special fees and permissions (*bribes and requests*).

The right to bare a second child is so expensive that only the very well-to-do and the very connected (*is there a difference?*) can possibly afford a second child.

This policy was directed primarily at urban-living people, those with a university degree, and those in low-level government employment. It does not cover, interestingly enough, the Uighur people who are strong proponents of large families due to their ninety-two percent Islamic and Christian following.

Fearing the Islamic resolve, Deng made certain that this policy would omit the Uighur people who are specifically identified in the new law.

The last thing he wanted was his *'still fragile'* hold on the people to be upset by radical Islam defending its right to propagate.

China had only recently lost hundreds of troops battling Uighur *'extremists'* in XinJiang Province in the oil-rich west of China. The Chinese came out much the worse in this conflict as their losses amounted to well over eight times those of the locals they had battled.

The ignominious defeat of the People's Liberation Army is largely a secret in China as is the massacre at Tiananmen Square in Beijing.

Only now, some thirty years after its enactment, have the horrors of this erroneous and draconian policy become fully visible.

One might say that the chickens have come home to roost. Today the results are myriad and serious. It's quite possible they are irreversible.

Despite this fact, the government recently boasted that they had *"... prevented the birth of over four hundred million unwanted ..."* This number amounts to the combined populations of the United States and the United Kingdom

This practice of ritualized and institutionalized slaughter has reaped horrible effects on China. It has inflicted damage far beyond that of the simple murders of the innocents and the desperate dissolution of the family.

A FAILED POLICY'S EFFECT ON THE ECONOMY. The Chinese economy has begun to grind down, slowing quarterly, and has only been saved by China's reluctant acceptance of millions of immigrants to fill vacant factory positions.

Despite the importation of millions of immigrants, China continues to lose manufacturing jobs as companies move their facilities out of China to India and South America. The shortage of workers has made conducting business untenable for many firms in China.

There also exists a burgeoning population of elderly in China. Because there are no children to replace them in the workforce, there is increasing difficulty in supporting the elderly. When they retire, it's the duty of the younger workers to provide funds to support their retirement.

As government officials have pretty well cleaned out the coffers, there is no *'money in the bank'* to support the elderly. A form of *'supply-side-finance'* has emerged where the money goes in one door and immediately out the other to finance such programs for now.

The numbers of elderly will soon be at parity with those of the young in China. This is tantamount to an economic Hydrogen Bomb!

Those implementing the policy thirty years ago failed to consider that one cannot have a rapidly growing economy when there aren't enough workers to keep the factories and businesses running.

With half of China's population living in the countryside as farmers, the government is afraid to allow them to fill these positions as the nation's food supply is the single critical element maintaining social order. Yes, through cheap, high quality, and readily available food, the people remain pacified.

JUVENILE CRIME ON THE RISE. This has jumped over eight hundred percent in the cities over just the past ten years. *This according to the Department of Public Safety in 2014.* The number of youths engaging in criminal activity or simple destructive delinquent conduct continues to climb.

When a child is born into a dual-income family, life as an *'only-child'* is the worst possible ingredient to fuel dissent and delinquent behavior.

With no siblings, inexperienced and often lazy parents, and a *'system'* afraid to offend them for fear of parental backlash in defense of their *'precious little sugar-pants'*, it doesn't look good.

JUVENILE MENTAL ILLNESS ON THE RISE. This has jumped precipitously. *This was a hard figure to track down but the Department of Public Health and Mental Retardation came up with it for me.*

It seems that, when a child is reared poorly enough, parents are all-to-quick to banish these *'bundles of joy'* to mental hospitals and 'special schools' in order to manage their behavior. *These children are often never seen again.*

A FAIRLY TYPICAL STORY. A parent walks along the footpath with her 8 year-old child in tow.

The boy is holding her hand (*many girls are aborted as soon as the sex is known, due to a heavy Oriental preference for boys which has resulted in a highly skewed male-female population ratio of nearly 2.3:1*).

As they walk, the first thing you notice is the 'Mom' is carrying his book bag and possibly also his musical instrument in its case.

They have come from or are going to classes. Again, 'Mom' is carrying the baggage as junior strolls along empty-handed. This form of coddling is all-too-common.

ANOTHER STORY. A parent and a child are in a fast food restaurant. Junior is wandering between tables, shouting aloud, and generally making an ass of himself. Mother is ordering lunch and grandmother is holding a table. The food is ready, and Mom carries it back to the table.

What ensues is a disgusting display of bad manners fueled by bad-rearing born of lazy parentage: The child jumps into a seat, knocking grandmother's bag off the table. He has also dislodged her glasses as she reacts to the sudden *'thump'* of his overfed and undisciplined body.

The boy gives her a look as if to say, *"Watch where you sit, old lady."* and the grandmother quietly tolerates this with her only response a smile and a timid, *"I'm sorry."* as she actually apologizes to the little shit. Mother sits by and does nothing.

The boy reaches, grabs, gulps, and makes farm-animal noises as he eats not only his own food, but from mother's and grandmother's plates as well.

Surprisingly, the mother reaches over, taking the boy's hand, and says, *"No. That's not how we behave in public."* I am nearly bowled over, but I know what's coming up next.

The boy throws his soft drink over his mother, calling her the Chinese word for *bitch'* and then he starts to cry. He is crying now because he has no soda to drink, having just soaked his mother with the old one as punishment for daring to challenge his command.

In anger over the lack of a soda, he knocks his food off the table onto the floor and begins a tirade that would match any you, in the west, have ever seen. ***Anybody got some Prozac?***

Mother and Grandmother sit by quietly, afraid to do anything, save to let *"Mommy's little sugar-pants"* get over it. Sadly, this is not at all an uncommon event.

Even more violent and inappropriate outbursts are quite common among Chinese adult society. It's clear that the children have quickly become the rulers of their domain in the home.

Through incessant and lavish coddling early in life, they have been taught by example that they are the center of the universe, and anything they want … they will damn well get!

RAMPANT JUVENILE INCOMPETENCE. This is an amazing thing to see, and it's everywhere!

- A mother wiping the nose of her twelve year-old son as he is helpless to do so, having never done it before except on his shirt sleeve.

- A mother laying out clothes for her sixteen-year-old before he goes to school or out to play.

- Even mothers spoon-feeding ten and twelve year-olds in public restaurants.

This level of coddling is dangerous in more ways than can possibly be printed. I have large numbers of university students (*almost always boys*) who cannot prepare a package of convenience noodles or sew a button on a shirt.

THE EXCEPTION IS. In Primary School, ready for these '*zoo animals*' teachers and administration in Primary Schools brace for each new batch every September.

Outbursts and misbehavior are dealt with harshly, quickly, and unerringly in a systematic series of punishments, examples, and close order drill on the parade ground to bring the students into line with required behavior in the Primary School System. Few things work better than a sound beating with a long stick, to restore order among the disorderly.

Within the first semester of Grade One, a child has been trained to behave appropriately (*at least in school*) *or that child has been shipped off to a school for the delinquent.*

Unfortunately, this system of behavior modification doesn't often carry over to the home and all-too-often the child releases the suppressed anger from school as soon as he or she gets home.

In this backlash tantrum, the target for these emotional hand grenades is anyone who gets in the way. Mom and Dad are left with bull's eyes on their chests.

GIRLS ARE GENERALLY THE EXCEPTION. Here is a different and entirely explainable situation. The 'unplanned' children of society, girls, are often governed by their parents with a much firmer hand and steady discipline than their male counterparts would ever see. The prejudice is obvious and prevalent.

Primary Schools rarely have behavior issues with little girls, and girls universally do better in school and other personal achievement than boys.

Gee, let me think, *"Boys do as they please from birth, while girls are disciplined from 'day-one'.* No wonder girls do so much better in life than their male counterparts.

Socially, academically, even professionally, girls excel in China with only society's and government's supreme prejudice against females standing in the way of otherwise unlimited growth and success.

While there exists a heavy predisposition of prejudice toward boys in the family, and in government employment, that is where it ends.

Socially, economically, in entry-level employment, and in education girls are preferred. As a professor in a prestigious university, and visiting professor in several others, I see immediately that the girls are the *'teachers' pets'.*

I, myself, would rather work in an all-girl environment in China. I see again and again that the boys are almost universally lazy, lethargic, undisciplined, and unrealistically hopeful of secure futures in the workforce.

The delusion of a Bachelor Degree being a 'ticket to the good life' exists even when faced with the undeniable fact that eighty-two percent of the 850,000 Bachelor Degree Graduates last year were still unemployed in December of the same year, that's six months later!

One thing this does well is to weed out the weaklings and the misfits. The few boys who apply themselves in school and have decent social skills and discipline almost always do extremely well upon graduation.

I recently went over a list of one hundred of my former students from the year before last. The girls generally found employment within ninety days of graduation and over eighty percent were employed in the field of their education. They were working in their major or in a closely related field.

The boys generally found employment within about six months of graduation and just under twenty percent were employed in the field of their education or a field related to their major.

That's just my own little survey, but it's indicative of the general situation.

TODAY IN THE 21st CENTURY. One sees the social damage done by this horrific One-Child policy. The laziness and stupidity of the workforce is now pretty much as it was during the Cultural Revolution.

By and large, the workforce is undisciplined, lazy, careless, and unmotivated.

Fortunately, this is now finally being recognized as a problem by corporate management as the spoon-fed ne'r-do-wells move from the labor force to the circles of management.

"We all rise to our own levels of incompetence."

FINAL CONCLUSION

Well, that about says it all. I live in a land riddled with inadequacy and criminal corruption on scales unimaginable to even a Chicago politician. They make the Daly administration look like The Salvation Army.

My life has been laid out before you and I have not held back. How I feel, what I feel, and why I feel are pretty well self explanatory in this tome.

I pray your understanding of those things written herein will be full and complete and that you may take home something useful and uplifting from what is written here.

Max Allen

THE END
for now ...

www.ingramcontent.com/pod-product-compliance
Lightning Source LLC
Chambersburg PA
CBHW072248310526
45795CB00011B/413